CW00485092

DreamSteps To Heaven

by
Jean Kelford

First published in Great Britain in 2008
by
Jean Kelford

Copyright © 2008 Jean Kelford

Names, characters and related indicia are copyright and trademark
Copyright © 2008 Jean Kelford

Jean Kelford has asserted her moral rights
to be identified as the author

A CIP Catalogue of this book is available from the British Library

ISBN 978-0-9558109-0-9

All rights reserved; no part of this publication may be reproduced or
transmitted by any means, electronic, mechanical, photocopying or
otherwise without the written permission of the publisher.

Printed and bound in
Great Britain by Biddles Ltd,
King's Lynn, Norfolk

DEDICATION

This book is in dedication to Professor Fowler, Doctor S Elniel, Doctor Raj and the team at the London Neurology and Neurosurgery Hospital who gave me my life back by operating and placing a Neurostimulator into my body to work my bladder, when I was found to be suffering with Fowlers Syndrome. The operation and the machine were a complete success, thank you. There are thousands and thousands of people who suffer with bladder complaints like mine and it quite literally stops them from getting on with their life. Thanks to the above hospital and people, help is at hand. Unfortunately they do not get a lot of funds for research or for helping patients who desperately need help, therefore I would like to help where I can and will be donating five percent of the royalties from this book to them by way of thanks to help them to keep up the good work and help others who are unfortunate enough to be in the position that I was in. My heartfelt thanks go to them.

FORWARD

I first met Jean when she brought my workplace to a standstill. Sitting in reception, and generally chatting about what she did, caused everyone passing by to stop and listen. They were absolutely fascinated. So was I - and I'll admit, I'm a self-confessed sceptic. But that didn't stop me from being interested in what she had to say - and the way she said it, can only be described as passionate. I've now known Jean for a number of years, and although that scepticism hasn't gone away (Jean admits that she loves sceptics!), I've seen her go from strength to strength, publishing ever more popular books, and organising ever more popular events. And that is one of Jean's unique qualities - the ability to communicate her subject like no other. The following pages, I'm sure, will be testament to that.

By Author and Journalist Andy Holmes.

CONTENTS

Introduction to
Dreamsteps to Heaven

Hello once again, readers everywhere. I always listen to what the readers of my books have to say to me because the purpose of my books is to make it easier for everyone to move forward in the belief that the Spirit World really does exist and is not just a figment of our imagination.

Something that has been said to me many times over by people after reading my second book,

"Is It You! Or is it Spirit?"

is that my readers have really enjoyed both my books but feel that it would be good if I could write some exercises for just one person in my next book. I understand that the reason for this is because a lot of people either live alone or else the people with whom they share their life either do not believe; do not have the time for or are frightened of the existence of the Spirit World. This book therefore has some exercises for one person included.

If only we realised from the beginning that our dreams were a way for us to lock into our intuitive side and therefore our ability to talk to the so-called dead, then I am sure that more people would share in a belief and talk to the people and animals in the Spirit World.

Because of this "Dream-steps to Heaven" has been written due to popular demand after it was indicated to me many times by readers of my previous books and listeners to me on the radio that people are very interested in finding out, not only what their dreams are saying to them but why? And also how they can tell if their dream is a message from

Spirit and what do they do to analyse their dream if it is.

I teach Spiritual Development in many places world wide, and always get asked the same type of questions. This therefore goes part of the way towards proving that people tend to have the same stumbling blocks when it comes to recognising the existence of the Spirit World.

For me teaching Spiritual Development is about people either here as everyone sees them, or in the next existence, which at the moment people have the impression is a gift that is only privy to a chosen few.

I am really lucky because my ability to link with 'the so-called dead' has been consistently polished throughout my experiences of life, even before I realised that I had a gift to do so.

In this book you will read more about my own experiences of living with the dead and the sometimes amazing or funny things that happen when those in the Spirit World feel an urgency to get their message across to us here. Sometimes hearing from that special person whom we feel has been lost to us for eternity is like a dream come true. It is so much so that Spirit frequently uses our dreams to reach us by writing a story in our hearts and minds for us to know what they are trying to tell us. Let me help you to understand what your dreams are telling you by helping you to analyse the stories created in your soul.

Owning **'Dreamsteps To Heaven'** and the Jean Kelford Dreamstep cards that go with the exercises in this book will help to make polishing your intuitive ability to link with your Guardian Angel and other Spirits easier to understand and handle, if nothing else.

You will find true stories and anecdotes about what peoples experiences with Spirit communication whilst asleep and awake are really about and other factors to do with communication from the Spirit World are included. Because this is book number three for me I also thought that it would be appropriate to include how both Spirit and the living can combine numerology (an ancient art) with the many other ways at their disposal to reach the hearts and minds of those of us who are still living.

From a very early age I would not only talk in my sleep but also sleepwalk too. This is because talking to the deceased was and is very natural to me, so to a person like me who is lucky enough to be born a natural Medium with a prominent gift for Spirit communication, it therefore becomes a real part of not only your waking hours but your sleeping hours too. This is why I would take notice of this communication and sometimes behave as though I was awake.

It appears that people are becoming more and more interested in anything to do with the subject of the Spirit World and one of the most confusing things to most people seems to be the fact that Spirit rarely speak in a voice that can be heard by all and make statements like my name is……. and I lived at………. This unfortunately leads someone who is already very sceptical or an outright non believer to say that there is no such thing as life after death.

As I have already stated, Spirit have many ways at their disposal with which to communicate with the living but unfortunately they all depend on the vibrational help of people here and the so called living. This may seem strange to many people but we have to accept that we as people have personal responsibility for our own lives here on our earthly vibration. Spirit, as such are not allowed to interfere with this unless we give them permission to do so. Although I should say that just a thought is enough of an indication to them.

For them to say my name is……. and I lived at…… takes a lot of energy from themselves and from you the recipient of the message they are trying to give communication to. This is purely because they need to vibrate the voice box of the person with whom they are trying to communicate in order to make the sound which becomes their voice. Remember they no longer live in our physical world so cannot use their own voice box because they are now wholly Spirit. We need to be totally relaxed to enable them to accomplish this sometimes difficult feat which means that most people do not quite get on the right vibration for long enough to hear a vocal statement regularly from Spirit. This is not for the want of trying on their part which is the reason why people attending Spiritualist meetings frequently have the desire to cough during the demonstration. This is because their loved ones are trying to talk to them directly instead of via the Medium, but getting in too close which presents the desire to cough for the recipient of the would-be message. For a Medium to hear clearly what the Spirit World is trying to say to the person here there needs to be a certain amount of co-operation from that person on a vibrational energy level. This does not mean that they have to already believe in the existence of the Spirit World but it does help if they are open to receiving the message whether they believe or not. A Medium however, can always give information that is accurate by describing what they see or sense from the Spirit visitor. This is just one of the explanations about how Spirit communication works that you will find in this book and others written by me.

As soon as we go into a sleepy state our vibration starts to change onto that same vibration where the Spirit World exist, this becomes even more heightened once we fall asleep. Remember even a sceptic loses their resolve to ignore and disbelieve in the existence of Spirit once they are asleep. This is the reason why sometimes a most ardent disbeliever will start to wonder after a vivid dream that has come to them from Spirit.

Our main problem with understanding and analysing our dreams is when our brain tries to change it into a dialogue that we will understand because it is received upside down and back to front, causing the dream and the message to become jumbled.

There are many dream dictionaries available on the market but people tend to just look up one aspect of their dream which does not un-jumble the information given in the original dream. If your brain is simply doing a bit of mental filing and sorting out the problems of the previous day, or you have simply eaten too heavily before bed and have had a restless night, then looking up one aspect of your dream would be fine but not if it is indeed Spirit communication to guide you in your life. This is because we need to correlate all aspects of the dream if it is Spirit communication and not just one single part of it. I am sure that you have all heard the saying: 'every picture tells a story' well this is so in the case of all dreams whether from Spirit or not.

If I was to show you a picture taken on my recent trip to the USA, you would just have a brief glimpse of where I was and maybe what I was doing at that time. Yet for me it would say a whole lot more. This is purely because the vibration of memory has been injected into my view of that photograph and what it meant to me. The same is so for dream communication from the Spirit World.

In other words what could be a common place occurrence, changes as soon as personal vibrations enter the scenario? This is so with dream communication. For instance seeing a flight of stairs becomes more than a stairwell as soon as you join together the position and any actions associated with that stairwell.

"Dreamsteps to Heaven" will help with this and many more Spirit linked communication methods which you are associated with. Questions like: Do you day dream? Are you sure that this is what you are doing? How do you know if something is a coincidence or Spirit sending their help? And many more questions are answered too. I would like to finish this introduction to what I hope you will find to be an interesting, educational and enjoyable read by telling you how Spirit communication can come in surprising ways that even a sceptic would have to consider strange.

Close friends of mine were unfortunate enough to need to attend the funeral of a close friend of theirs recently. Whilst there they asked what would happen to their friend's bungalow because he had no living relatives. Although they did not find out straight away, they later learned that his home was to go up for auction, so decided to buy it if they could.

After successfully buying the property at auction Pat and George happily went to collect the keys. They had trouble finding somewhere to park and had not got much time to spare so they parked on the pay and display but because they had only to cross the road to pick up the keys and the parking machine was at the other end of the car park they decided to risk it. Unfortunately the keys were not where they should have been and they had to walk to the other end of the town to fetch them. I know that you have already realised that they got back to find a forty pound parking ticket on the car window.

When they got back to the bungalow itself it had been totally cleared before it went up for sale so stood empty and they were reminiscing about their friend the late owner. George started work almost immediately on preparing it for the renovations that they were going to do to their newly acquired home. All the drawers in the kitchen had been emptied so he took them outside and much to his surprise when he went to pull a plank of wood off the bottom of the cupboard under where the drawers had been; it came off in his hand. There inside was a false drawer and in it were a few items including £39.80 pence in cash plus a £5 coin. They smiled to themselves and said thank you to their friend for the money to pay the fine.

What do you think? Coincidence!! I believe the cash which was twenty pence short of the fine was his way of bringing them luck for their new home. They needed to receive the fine in order to see the coincidental way it happened and due to the fact that the money was twenty pence short which is not a great deal and remember they did also find the five pound coin. This indicates that if they keep the five pound coin he will see to it that they will always have enough money for their needs. Good don't you think!!!

Chapter One
The Wonder of Spirit

1

The Wonder of Spirit

Standing on a rostrum like the one you will find in most Spiritualist Churches or on a stage in a theatre or somewhere like that, is an experience in itself, but it is only a small part of being a Medium. There are obviously lots of different things involved if you hold the title Medium. These include linking the two worlds; healing, teaching Spiritual development, clearing ghosts from haunted places which involves sending lost Spirits home to the light, or convincing mischievous Spirits that they need to leave the person or place they are staying attached to here, and go home to the comfort and love which is the Spirit World where they now reside, and of course all manner of other things too.

Being a Medium is all about linking with Spirits both incarnate and discarnate or in other words, alive or dead. By alive I mean that every living soul has a Spirit from the moment of conception. This is the part of us that decides what type of character we have. This Spirit is capable of communicating with ourselves and to others via vibrations which are special to us personally.

As I have stated before in a previous book, sometimes people speak at a person instead of to them. For instance they do this by saying: "Hello how are you?" then without listening to their reply they carry on with either a separate conversation or else they move on their way to wherever they were heading at the time they bumped into you. Whereas, if we listen closely to that person and what they are saying, we will not only listen to their reply but tune into the vibration of their Spirit too. This is done by listening to what they are not saying. In other words, just because a person answers the question: "How are you?" with "I am fine thank you" it does not necessarily mean that everything is rosy in their world. They may be replying in this way because they do not think that you will want to be bored with their problems. The English language for instance is open to many interpretations from the same simple sentences and I am sure that the same can apply in all languages including the language of the Spirit World when they try to communicate with us.

This talent of reading the vibrations given off by the living is very important when portraying a message from the Spirit World because sometimes people can misunderstand what we are trying to say to them, thereby misinterpreting what their loved one in the Spirit World is trying to send out in their direction. This is always sad for both the person receiving the message and the Spirit visitor. When we speak to Spirits who have already passed over to the Spirit World we do the same thing, which is read their vibration. A Medium also needs to be aware that the Spirit visitor is doing exactly the same thing. They are both reading, and tuning in to our vibration to portray their message and to let a Medium know exactly whom their communication is for. This is one of the main reasons why they make use of the subliminal part of our brain as explained in my previous book 'Is It You. Or is it Spirit.' This is a very real part of our brain that works silently on our behalf to inform us of things that we should be aware of.

The subliminal is part of our physical body that relies on our Spirit to work properly. Spirit have to communicate with the living by making use of any ways open to them because even when people are capable of linking with the Spirit side of life, they sometimes are personally not aware of it. For instance children who are invariably capable of communicating with the dead but do not realise that they have this ability, quite often lose this talent as they become older because of the fact that it has not been acknowledged by those around them and therefore becomes latent. My Granddaughter Leah is a classic example of a child having the ability to link to the Spirit World, but fortunately in her case it will be encouraged so therefore it will develop.

I visited her on the day of her eighth birthday two years ago and she was telling me about her bedroom in their new home. She told me that she sometimes woke up in the night and could see two eyes staring at her from over by the curtain. I of course realised that this was a Spirit visitor who was watching over her, but knew that I needed to be careful how I explained this because of her age. I did not want to frighten her any more than she already appeared to be. I thought for a moment, and then said in a gentle voice:

"Do not worry sweetheart it was probably only Uncle Jack."

I said this knowing I had already explained to her in the past that her uncle Jack lived in the Spirit World now and would still visit and watch over her, even though most of the time she would not be able to see him. She immediately replied:

"No Nanny, it can't be Uncle Jack because he had blue eyes and that man had!!"

At this she momentarily looked up into the air then almost straight away said:

"Hazel eyes."

We people in the room all looked at one another because you have to admit that you would not expect an eight year old to give hazel as a colour. I then asked her if she knew what a vibration is, to which she gestured a gentle waving movement of her hand from side to side and answered:

"Is it when it goes sort of like that?"

We all laughed and I told her that she had got the general idea and went on to explain about how Spirit live in the same space as we do but on a much faster vibration and this means that we cannot always see the Spirit visitors. However, sometimes when we are relaxed like we are when we have been to sleep we are on the right vibration to see them. I also explained that it took a lot of love for Spirit to visit us which meant that the man whom she frequently saw in her bedroom would not want to hurt her.

Her next reply was:

"Well why do I sometimes see a funny mist like stuff in my room?"

I tried to give her the explanation of the fact that this was due to ectoplasm forming because Spirit were about to appear without giving her too much information at such a tender age. She then enquired: "Is that why, whenever I come down the stairs, I feel as though there is someone following me?" I explained that this was only her Guardian Angel following her around to look after her. She seemed happy with this explanation and the subject was changed for the time being, because you should never pressure, or allow young children to talk about Spirit for too long in one go, because if you do they just start to invent things because their imagination kicks in. She did ask me one last question as I was leaving to go home later that evening which was:

"Nanny why do I only see Spirit when I am sad?"

Good point! This is because we change our vibration and draw inwards when we are sad which puts us on the right vibration to see Spirit, just as she did. Although I would also like to point out that when we are really happy the energy from that happiness can also change our vibration onto the one where the Spirit World reside.

As I said in the introduction you would be amazed at the ways in which those we love in the Spirit World grab our attention at times, here are just a few of the amazing things that they do to let us know they are here. I was attending the funeral of a good friend and very Spiritual man called Bill Kitson on Tuesday 26th July 2005 when he did something that brings back a reminder from the other side of life of just how Spiritual and kind he is. The really special service that was held at Stirchley Spiritualist

Church for Bill was going really well and was approximately half way through. I had managed to this point with just the occasional tear of sadness for our loss of this special man. I underwent major surgery two and a half weeks earlier for a total knee replacement which was still extremely painful at this point. Although I should have still been at home resting my leg, I felt that there was no way I would miss Bill's funeral so therefore was sitting very carefully watching that nobody knocked my already throbbing leg, when Bill who had been standing at the front of the Church near to where his wonderful wife Muriel, and family were seated, suddenly walked down the central aisle of the Church kissed me on the cheek and said, "Are you okay Jean?" At this I burst into instant tears. It is hard to believe that there Bill was, attending his own funeral and he took time out to make sure that I was alright. This shows true Spirituality right to the end.

After leaving the Church to head for Telford Crematorium where the remainder of the service was to be held, my husband Mike, friend Chris and I were not sure where to go and I saw a man leave whom I had spoken to at the service and suggested that Chris who was driving, should follow him to the Crematorium. We had been travelling for a few minutes when as we crossed an island to turn right we noticed that the funeral cars were waiting to cross behind us, from the road on the left as they had travelled a different way. We laughed at this because it looked as if we were ahead of the funeral. We decided that once there we could wait in the car park for their arrival so carried on tailing the man who had been to the first part of the funeral service. However, at that point the car that we were following turned onto the M54. I instantly said:

"I don't think he is going to the funeral service after all"

But too late Chris had followed him onto the motorway. We had no choice but to travel to the next exit which was a long junction then make our way back to find the Crematorium. We arrived just as the service was about to recommence and there was Bill at the front standing by his coffin giving us a knowing grin. He had a wonderful sense of humour and I am sure he saw the funny side of what had happened and I also find it interesting that because of the extra journey I got the chance to rest my bad leg for a while between services, so my pain had eased a little. Coincidence!!! I do not think so, do you? I will leave it to you to decide but I know what I believe.

We later found out that the man whom we had been following was heading home for Walsall where he lived. Chris also lives in Walsall so I asked if she had any relationship to homing pigeons! I thought that you would find it interesting and funny to hear that it is not the first time that Chris has become confused at a funeral. She once accidentally attended the wrong funeral. It is a good job that she is learning to communicate with the dead, don't you think. Then in many years time when it is her funeral, hopefully she will be there on time and at the right one!!!

Two days after Bill's funeral, I met up with some of my closest friends and we were communicating with Spirit. The four of us, Chris, Laureece, Lucy and I, were linking with Spirit and we were suddenly given "I am pleased, it will be at the Edge at Much Wenlock. We did not understand this information but assumed that it was a place, Spirit were talking about. The following Sunday, I conducted the service at Stirchley Spiritualist Church. Bill's wife Muriel attended the service during which I gave her a communication from her husband Bill. After the service she came to thank me and said, "I have got his ashes back and we are going to scatter them at the edge at Much Wenlock" on Wednesday because he was born in Much Wenlock. Both Chris and I looked at one another as our mouths fell open with surprise and we all agreed that the incident was amazing and gave a lot of proof of Bill's survival after death to us all, me included.

I was in the Doctors waiting room for my turn to see the Phlebotomist to have my blood taken. Mike was sitting next to me and there was a lady whom we did not know sitting directly opposite where I was seated. I was looking at the lady because she was extremely well tanned and I was wondering whether she had been away or not, when suddenly a lady from the Spirit world appeared standing next to her.

As I looked at the Spirit visitors eyes I distinctly heard the tune 'This is the dawning of the Age of Aquarius' being played over and over in my head. Normally under these circumstances I would have ignored this information because I do not connect people with Spirit unless asked to do so because I believe this to be leaky Mediumship. However, on this occasion I felt that it was necessary to speak to her so I told her that I kept hearing the tune:

'This is the dawning of the Age of Aquarius'

played repeatedly in my head each time that I looked at her. She instantly replied:

"Well I am an Aquarius, so perhaps you are getting vibes."

I in turn explained that I was a Medium to which she replied:

"Well carry on then give me some more."

I answered that I did not usually do that in places like Doctors waiting rooms, to which she retorted "but I have asked you to, so please go on and tell me more." I explained that there was a lady standing next to her from Spirit and gave her a description of the lady who said she was her mother and how she had died. Her mother gave her some advice on a situation around her at that time and said "I want to help you because today is special and I wish that I had done what I wanted when I was here on the earth and not what other people thought that I should do." The lady's mouth fell open as she said, "I do not believe in all this because I am a Catholic but I am an Aquarius. Your description of my mother and how she died is spot on and it is a special day because it is the anniversary of her death, it is twelve months today since she died. I am totally gob smacked." Yet again Spirit, have managed to surprise me and amaze and please a total non believer with their wisdom.

On another occasion whilst holding a private sitting for a very psychically gifted man called Richard, and his mother, I was made aware of a chocolate factory. I told him that this did not feel totally right to me and I felt that it was more likely to do with a catering type business venture that he would be involved with. I felt that the chocolates to be sold would be made at home, but felt that it had something to do with Gloucester. (Both Richard and I naturally assumed this was the place.) As I have stated before we should never assume anything when communication comes from Spirit, but I am human aren't I? I went on to relay that I could also see Richard in those big old fashioned type buildings in London, like where the embassies are. The day after I gave the pair their readings, they went to have a look at a business in Dorridge. A sandwich bar which Richard told me, on paper looked great….. The very first thing, that caught his eye in the display counter were three boxes of hand made chocolates!!!! On questioning the young man who served them (remember he did not know why Richard and his Mum were there), he said that the owners were losing money hand over fist and were looking to sell!!!! End of story you might think, however, the following Saturday they had been invited to go and see Cirque du Soleil at the Royal Albert Hall with eight other members of their family. Richard told me that it was great and they all enjoyed walking round the beautiful streets that surround the Hall.

On their way back, they had to get the tube at South Kensington and the train was packed (5.30pm on a Saturday afternoon.).... Everyone trundled along to get to an almost empty carriage but because Richard had lived in London, and being at the back of their party, he realised that he would not get on the train unless he darted to the next door, still for the same carriage but at the other end. Everyone thought that he had missed the train but he had managed to get a standing place….. He then told me that right in front of his eyes was a card that had been wedged at eye level advertising whey protein…. Available from a place called **THE CHOCOLATE FACTORY**…. Slightly more bizarre was the fact that they had just pulled into **GLOUCESTER ROAD** tube station. After this Richard decided to refine his search for his new business to London!!! Spirit know how to get their message across to us when they need to, don't you think?

Recently my eldest daughter Dawn was staying with us for a few days and because all the beds were taken Dawn slept downstairs on one of the sofas. I had been out working as usual and arrived home with Chris at about 11.30pm. As we walked into the house and the lounge we were as quiet as possible because all the people in the house were in bed (including Dawn on the sofa) and were more than likely asleep. As we stepped inside the lounge door, Dawn popped her head up from under the duvet and said hello. Chris and I stood at the end of the sofa where Dawns feet were situated so that we could talk to her for a while before Chris headed for home and me of course to bed.

The conversation did not take long to get around to Spirit and Chris enquired of Dawn if she would like to be a Medium one day. Dawn immediately retorted:

"Well! yes and no."

All three of us laughed at this reaction and of course if there is laughter about then you can be sure that Spirit will let their presence be known. We all went cold and Dawn remarked that although she was one hundred percent certain that Spirit and the afterlife exist, she was not sure whether it would frighten her too much to be aware of them clearly whilst I was not with her. She carried on to say:

"if something moved now when you are both with me it would give me the spooks enough and maybe frighten me."

True to form at precisely that moment, the standard lamp that was situated by the side of the sofa and therefore at that moment behind Dawns head switched off with the timer. Dawns face was a treat as she shot up and called:

"Help!!"

She had been made aware earlier that week what time the timer switched the lamp off but had not considered two factors. One was that she was so engrossed in our conversation that she had forgotten all about the lamp and consequently the fact that the timer would switch it off at all, let alone at that moment. Secondly she did not give credit to the fact that the clocks had been altered the previous night and therefore the lamp switched off an hour earlier than it had the previous night because the timer had not yet been changed to catch up with things. It is interesting though, don't you think, that Spirit altered the atmosphere of the room shortly before the timer activated and the light went out. They were obviously listening and wanted to create a reaction which they did. Should I ask:

"Where were you when the lights went out?"

One evening, at about 11.30pm after Chris and I had arrived at my home from a Spiritualist Church where I had been addressing the congregation with a service. Chris made a drink to take upstairs to bed for me before she left because I had in recent times had major surgery on my leg and could not manage to take things upstairs myself. As she climbed onto approximately the fourth stair there was a sudden noise as though someone was walking upstairs. Because Chris thought that it was my husband Mike going across the landing to the toilet and was not sure whether he would be adequately dressed for her to see him, she did a swift and sudden turn about and came a cropper, tumbling down the stairs and although managing to at least stay on her feet and not hurt herself she promptly threw part of the cup of hot chocolate that she was carrying, up the wall. I rushed into the hallway as fast as my bad leg would allow me to, only to find that she had worried for nothing because it was Spirit walking about upstairs and not Mike at all, because as it turned out he was fast asleep in bed.

My friend Simone wrote a poem about a lady after being made aware of her grave on a visit to New Zealand, before finding out that the lady in question was her Spirit guide. (You can read the full story in my last book. "Is It You! Or Is It Spirit?") Simone then decided to immigrate to New Zealand, which she did on Easter Bank Holiday Monday of last year.

Two days later on the Wednesday evening I was with a group of friends and we were linking to Spirit, so we all switched off our mobile phones so as not to be disturbed which is usual practice when linking in to the Spirit World. We all turned them off at the same time to make sure that none of us forgot. Approximately one hour after we had started work, my mobile phone bleeped and flashed as if a text message had come in, which totally shocked all that were present because they had all been witness to the fact that I had switched it off before the Spirit linking procedures had started. I of course picked my telephone up with the intention of turning it off so that we could carry on with the work we were doing. However, everyone there agreed that my mobile was in fact still switched off!!!

We therefore decided that perhaps I had better turn it on and check the text message in case Spirit, were trying to draw my attention to something. Once on the phone indicated that there was indeed a text message and it was from Simone, I quickly checked and this is what it said:

'I am here in New Zealand and really need some words of encouragement, feeling very scared and home sick. X'

We of course decided that it was fairly urgent and we decided that I should answer the text to reassure Simone before we returned to work. Can I just add that if I did not hear that message come in at that time, I would not have switched my phone back on until at least midnight? The call came in at 8.55pm our time. Simone is in fact extremely psychic as these two incidents go part way to prove, and Spirit knew that it was important for me to acknowledge that even though we were now living many miles apart, Spirit and I were in fact there for her as I had promised we would be. This was Spirit working their wonders again when it was most needed.

DREAMSTEPS TO HEAVEN

Chapter Two

New Guides and the Way They Work With Us

2

New Guides and the Way They Work With Us

Sometimes working with Spirit is very straightforward whilst at other times it can be quite puzzling, but one of the things that a Medium learns very quickly is not to take our Spirit visitors for granted. Going back to the year 2003, my week had been a very mixed one where our work with Spirit had been concerned. I had recently acquired a new guide whom appeared to be a bit of a comedian. This is evident by the way that whenever he showed himself during a service or sitting, I found myself saying increasingly funny things whilst still giving a high standard of evidence of proof of survival. I should explain that whilst we have certain guides that are with us all our lives, there are also those who join us at certain points in our learning pattern of linking with 'the so called dead?' This new guide had obviously been introduced to me at this stage in my learning because they felt that I was ready for the type of knowledge that he was able to impart and also because of the fact that there had been a few sad things happening around me in my everyday life at that time and taking notice of the fact that my health was not very good either, they felt that his comical input would be well timed? I would have to agree with them on this one.

My new Guide was to be a gentleman who had a Lancashire accent, and was approximately five feet eight inches tall, with a receding hairline. He was a little over weight around the middle and he tended to laugh quite a lot. One Sunday whilst Mike and I were conducting a service in front of about fifty-six people, (Mike used to work alongside me) my new Guide put in an appearance. This meant that during the whole of the evening the people in the congregation were falling about laughing as were we.

He has a quaint way of phrasing things, which if I am wise I will think about before repeating his information word for word? During one communication from the other side I was very aware of a lady in the Spirit world who was of an extremely friendly temperament. I asked her for more information so that I could introduce her to the recipient of the messages at that time. In answer to this she showed me a clear picture of herself making sausages on this little machine that was putting the sausage meat into the skins, and spinning the skin around between the separate links of sausage? He, however, immediately told me to say: "Do you understand a lady here who links to sausage-making?" I of course repeated this, before realising what I was in fact saying? I then laughed and asked if they realised what I had just said saying: "Links to sausage making?" Everyone in the room was in fits of laughter including myself. After this point the evidence of proof of survival was very strong and easy to give and receive, which is after all the point of the subject. Laughter you see, raises the vibrations in the room and as Spirit are on a much higher vibration than us, it makes it easier for them to communicate with us. As we sat down after finishing our part of the service, I went to place my glasses on the table in front of me, and had a spasm in my hand causing me to throw my spectacles over my shoulder onto the floor behind my chair. Once again laughter rang out as I retorted: "I am safe you know?"

You may be thinking: 'What has me throwing my glasses got to do with the Spirit world?' However, I should point out that although as I have explained in my previous books, I do have a tendency to have spasms when my calcium levels are low, which they were that day, obviously causing this mishap. The glasses had been thrown quite a way, landing behind the chairs on the hard floor sliding along as they did so, yet they were undamaged or marked, which was an amazing coincidence; especially when you consider that my new guide had taken his glasses off and thrown them at the same time, to make a point that he had been involved.

One evening, my Brother Keith and his lovely fiancée Dawn, came to our house because we were all going out for a meal. When he went to sit on our settee, he noticed something on the cushion. Before taking his seat he picked up the object, and handing it to me said: "Here you are Sis. I don't know what this is, but it was on your sofa?" He handed me a small gold coloured plastic rune with the letter M printed on it. I need to say at this junction in time that I had been given a set of runes like the one he had found, three years earlier, as part of a Christmas present. The odd part was that I had not seen them for almost the amount of time that I had owned them, yet one of them had shown up that day in our lounge? I am not certain where the rest of the set is but I suspect that they are upstairs in our home office? Spirit had obviously materialised the rune to where it was found to make a point? When you also consider that at that time I was concerned about a close friend of mind whom I care about very much, and was not in touch with, and his initial is M, then it all starts to become clear, doesn't it?

The evening that Mike and I spent with my Brother and his girlfriend was a really enjoyable one. We were sitting chatting, whilst having a coffee after returning from the restaurant when Keith's face contorted into a serious expression, as his lips went into a whooo shape. He retorted: "Did you hear that?" All three of us answered at the same time: "Hear what?" At this he shuddered as he told us that someone had laughed from behind him on his left hand side by the lounge door? We all laughed at this as I said: "I told you didn't I? That was Dad you heard laughing because he is here with us" Keith shuddered again at this and we all had a good laugh at his expense. About ten minutes later he pulled a funny face once more and grabbing Dawn's hand said: "Did you see that then?" She simply replied: "You mean the clock?" He in turn assured her that 'yes' this is what he had been talking about? We had a statue clock on a court cupboard at the opposite end of the room to where they were sitting together on the sofa at that time. The clock part swung from side to side in rhythm, as a statue of two ladies hold it up in the air. They, however, had seen the clock stop swinging as though someone was holding it still, shudder and then start to swing normally. This happened twice, but the second time I saw it too. However, I could see my Father stop it and hold it still for a second before releasing it, whereas they could only see the clock's actions because they were not able to see our Dad who is in Spirit. It was obviously more disconcerting for the pair of them because they were not used to everyday communication with Spirit and how they work, as Mike and I were. Once again the laughter factor was being used because of the presence of my new guide who tells me his name is: 'Sid Woods.'

Many months later I was demonstrating and had been giving messages to a group of people who were new to Spiritualism, when I told a gentleman that his Grandmother whom I described was calling out a name. I gave the name, which he said was his daughter's name. Then I said: "I presume this lady has been in prison a long time." As soon as I realised what I had said, I corrected it and retorted: No she hasn't been in prison at all, she has been in Spirit a long time." The whole place went up with laughter as he accepted what I was saying. I then told them that sometimes because I am listening to lots of conversations from people who are in Spirit I get a bit ahead of myself and repeat part of the next piece of the communication before I have finished what I am saying. In the same way I sometimes leave off the end of the sentence when I am talking to someone in the living World without realising it, because I hear Spirit saying it and think the person whom I am talking to has heard it too. I then explained that the subject of prison had come up for one of the group, and I would talk to them about it in a moment. Me being me after I had finished the link I was on, I went on to give a message to someone new across the other side of the room before realising and coming back with a message for another lady in the group who worked for the prison service.

One Sunday evening Mike and I arrived at Brownhills Excelsior Church to conduct the evening service, and were escorted to a little room out the back to sit and have a cup of coffee before the service commenced. Two close friends were with us that evening and came through to the little room with us for a few minutes. As we were sitting talking, my main guide Mr R suddenly walked around Mike who was sitting on my right hand side, and positioned himself standing by Mike's right shoulder, which was about the same position that he normally stood by me. I was surprised by this because it was something that he did not usually do. I told Mike and the girls what had happened, and we all laughed as one friend commented: "Perhaps he can see that Mike is really nervous?", which to be fair he was, as was I. This was after all, a normal state of affairs, as we were preparing ourselves to start any service with Spirit.

This incident was forgotten for the time being, when the chairperson came to talk to us about the order of service for that evening, I explained that it may be necessary for me to come off the rostrum at some point during the service because of the fact that I wore a surgical bag at that time after recent surgery, and this bag sometimes became very full and needed emptying, especially as I would be drinking a lot of water during the service which was normal practice for me at this time also. This is purely because Spirit work well close to water. I explained to her that if it became necessary for me to leave during the service, then I would wait until Mike was linking before I did so? She said that this was okay but told me to sit in the chair on her right near to the door, because the rostrum is narrow and I would find it difficult to get off from the other side, should it become necessary.

I chose not to say anything under the circumstances, but the truth is that I would have been happier being on the opposite side of the rostrum, with Mike on my right, which was our normal position whilst working. My reason for this preference is purely because Mr R always stands on my right because that is where any person's Guardian Angel always stands to be in the best position for linking with us? If Mike also stood on my right, it then meant that Mr R would be positioned standing between the two of us. This enables him to keep a close watch on any links that my husband is making should I forget momentarily because I am linking elsewhere. Our positioning on the rostrum that evening however, meant that Mr R was still standing between the two of us, but was on Mike's right and my left. He knew that I was experienced enough for this not to make any difference to the quality of my links, and he was right.

It amazed us all that evening because although I was feeling unwell, I usually do not notice this factor if it occurs whilst I am working. That day however, I was suffering quite a lot and decided to allow Mike to make most of the links, which as I said is unusual for me. In fact he usually has trouble getting a word in edgeways, because I tend to forget him once I am occupied linking with Spirit. It was not until the next day that my friend had asked me whether this was the reason my guide had moved around to Mike's right, in order to let me know not to worry that he would still be keeping an eye on him for me? The answer is a very definite yes. As I have said before sometimes Spirit still manage to surprise me and this was one of those instances. Something else that was noticeable that evening was that Mike seemed to work with a lot more confidence than he normally did, which obviously bodes well for the future.

Sometimes working with Spirit, just like life itself, is a mixture of great joy and sadness at the same time. This has to be so, for us to follow the pathway that we are here for, which is to learn lessons that will further our own Spirit and in turn the World as we know it. Even for someone of my experience working with those from the other side! It can be difficult to understand what lesson you are supposed to be learning from any experience that repetitively and apparently randomly comes your way. But once you start to be aware of your own soul and what it is calling out to you, the whole subject of why certain things happen to us becomes more obvious and clear.

Things are repeated so that we will be more likely to notice them. This is a form of sublimated message used to make us sit up and take notice of something or someone affecting changes in our life either for the better or worse that we are taking no notice of. This is basically because if we miss the things that can change our lives for the better or worse we will never move forward but stay rigidly static where we are. Those opportunities of things to improve our lives or stop bad things taking hold of circumstances around us will then be missed and sometimes you only get "one bite of the cherry," so to speak. This means that if something happens and it is presented a second time so that you can change the order of events then you may not get a third chance so it is good to notice it and make use of your opportunity to alter the events as they occur if this is what you want to do. Things are never as random as they would appear. There is a reason for everything, and all things can be turned around to put positive influences into our lives and make things better for us.

The rule applies here that if something happens more than once the Spirit World is trying to indicate to you that there is something that you either should be doing and are not, or should not be doing but are. These actions inadvertently stop you from learning one or more of the lessons that you are here to learn or at least slows down its application into your life pathway, thereby diverting your attention into a different direction which is not as good for you or your life. If something occurs three or more times then it is urgently time for you to take notice of the information that you are being given.

As I am sure I have already said before, I can be the worse culprit for ignoring messages that are repeated within my Aura and therefore my life. I am actively working on changing this at this time in my life. I will give you an example of what I mean: When I was younger and I was due to get married for the first time, I was uncertain that it was the right thing to do but because circumstances declared that one of my younger brothers was to die just before the wedding took place, I was left trying to differentiate between the sad feelings that I was having because of the overwhelming grief that I was dealing with, and the happy feelings that should have been there because of my approaching wedding day. The right thing to do would have been to postpone the wedding until I could understand my feelings and emotions better, but me being me, I ignored this overwhelming feeling of, Whoa wait, and instead worried about what other people were thinking and feeling about it all. Because of this, common sense went out of the window, and I ignored my much to be relied upon intuition that was telling me, "no slow down and wait a while."
I repeated this same pattern with my second marriage when my stepdaughter passed away just before my wedding day, which had

been brought forward in the first place because she was quite poorly at that time. I should have learned my lesson the first time, that it is impossible to understand our feelings properly when we are dealing with two opposite emotions at the same time. On reflection, once again, we should have postponed. This would have given us both time to sort out what was happening deep within our souls and act accordingly, thereby allowing us to enjoy our choices more. I am not telling you that either of these marriages was wrong for me, because good and bad lessons occur on every pathway we choose to take. However, if your emotions are in turmoil, it might be wise to postpone for a while, because once you have taken the decision to follow a certain course of action and go through with it your way of life is diverted in that direction, so therefore you should take the time to make sure that it is right for you because there is no going back to that point in your life without carrying the experiences of that pathway with you wherever you go in this life.

This is where the saying that he or she is carrying "baggage" with him or her takes place. An interesting point is that as soon as we are able to understand a little about right and wrong, good and bad, we start to accumulate this so called "baggage." Remember, even a three year old gets personal responsibility for how they interact with those around them. My Granddaughter when she was almost three years old was told to come along because it was time for her bath, to this she answered: "No thank you Mummy I don't want to." Without letting her hear we laughed about this, because although it was technically naughty to say 'no' to her Mum, you have to admire her for the sweet and polite way which she did it. So you see, even at this tender age she had grasped the idea that it is important to try to do what you want to do whilst taking account of other people's feelings at the same time. I think maybe she is a chip off the old block don't you? However she is learning much quicker than her Nan did!

You should never worry that you are being selfish with any actions that you are about to take or have taken because the truth is that you are here to follow your pathway and as such you have personal responsibility for what you and only you do. We cannot take responsibility for anyone else's actions and should never try because this would mean that we have failed to learn one of the biggest lessons in our life. This is, to live our life in the way which gains us the entrance onto any pathway that will enhance our life and therefore the lives of others.

The lesson for me in these two almost identical situations was, to occasionally spend a little time thinking about the following questions:

Is this really what I want to do at this moment in time?

Am I doing it for me or for others?

If I am doing it for others, will it adversely affect my own life if I go ahead with my present plans?

Will I be happy with the consequences of my actions?

For following your intended life pathway, our answers to these questions should be:

YES.

FOR MYSELF.

NO.

YES.

If however you feel that at the time that you are trying to make these decisions you are not sure how you feel, or you swap from one decision to another, then you should wait because your soul is calling out to you that it would be a mistake to make that decision at this time.

Those of you, who have read my previous books, will already be aware that my reason for diverting our attention from Spirit linking to everyday life and its decision making is because the two are always closely linked together. Spirit always uses the information that we know and rely upon when attempting to relay any information about themselves for someone here on the earth. This is why we should never bring what is taking place in our lives at that time into the scenario of Spirit linking. People who know me well would agree that if I am having problems in my private life and am feeling sad and/or down, once I start work you would never spot that there were in fact any problems around me at all. This is the way it should be because if I stand in front of a congregation of people and am aware of my own sadness, how am I supposed to recognise a sense of sadness for the person here from the Spirit World or in fact from the Spirit themselves.

Just like in life one thing that the would-be Medium should always look out for, is any repetitive action because this is always confirmation that the Medium has picked the message up correctly. If the person here starts to cry upon receiving a message from their loved one in Spirit it is always a good sign, because it means that something in the information the Spirit World has portrayed to them through you has touched deep within their soul. This tells us that the magnets within the Aura of the recipient of the message have ignited their Spirit in that brief moment, to bring about a shudder of hope and happiness that their loved one does in fact live on and has not just disappeared into the Abyss for ever and ever. This is in fact because the soul of the person they love in the Spirit World has touched their own soul and caused it to light up in that brief instant of recognition. This is the reason why in this instance it is considered to be okay to make someone cry.

We tend to associate tears with sadness and laughter with happiness but it is not always as clear-cut as that. I cried whilst my daughters were getting married because of how beautiful they looked. I cried with pride when my children and grandchildren were born because I was so happy. I cried recently when someone told me how proud they were to know me, because it meant that they could see my achievements in life, and how hard they had been for me to come by. So you see these are just a few examples of where I cried because I was happy.

On the other side of the coin, any one who knows me well will tell you that I like to laugh and to hear other people laugh. This comes, I am sure, from the fact that the Spirit world, make their presence known much more easily by touching against the magnets within our Aura and causing a spark of recognition of something or someone good being nearby when the vibrations around us are raised with laughter. I cannot claim to have known that this was what was happening back in my childhood days but I very quickly learned the lesson that if I made people laugh there seemed to be more people and more happiness around.

Perhaps we should all try this regularly because at the very least it would make the world and our life in it a better place to be.

That is one side of laughter but as I explained with crying it is not always as clear-cut as that. Close friends laugh at me because if I get very nervous or surprised by things that are taking place I burst out laughing. I know that this reaction sounds strange but it is a part of me. I think that this is because at these times I tend to open out my Aura wider and this makes me vulnerable to any dangers around me.

When I was a young girl at school in the juniors, my close friend found my laughter to be more of a curse than something comical although she always laughed about it later. This is because when it was time for Art class our work desk where we shared projects was facing the wall at the back of the classroom in the left hand corner of the room, which meant that we had our backs to the rest of the class and of course to the teacher. My friend was always messing about and although I was giggling I used to get nervous in case the teacher saw us and we got into trouble. This always served to make me laugh out loud and we always ended up cleaning out the Art stockroom for the afternoon as a punishment.

If I am working with physical Mediumship and I am suddenly made aware that Spirit are about to do something like lift the table and I know that the other people in the group have not noticed I cannot help but laugh with excitement at the prospect of what is about to happen. So you see, at times I find it difficult to hold back laughter for all sorts of reasons, and not just because I am happy or something really funny has taken place. My reason for telling you all this is because if you look at the different and sometimes unusual quirks to do with your nature you will find that there are probably ways with which you are already linking in to the energy created by a Spirit World that perhaps you claim not to be aware of!!!

Only recently, I Jean Kelford, professional Medium, did not understand what was happening when Spirit were trying to bring about recognition of something that they were trying to make me aware of. This was simply because I was working very hard and did not have time for idle chatter outside my work perimeters. It all started one morning whilst I was at a bookshop to do a book signing and give demonstrations. I was suddenly aware of a buzzing sensation in my left nipple. This happened several times during that morning, until finally I told my friend Chris about it and she asked "should you go to the doctors?" I answered that this was not necessary because I was not ill. The buzzing sensation did not hurt at all, it was just a funny fuzzy feeling that was there from time to time but was in my Aura rather than my physical body. That was when I came to the conclusion that it might be Spirit trying to catch my attention.

This went on for several days then finally stopped as suddenly as it had started. However, this was not the end of the matter, in fact it was just the beginning because a few nights later I was woken up from my sleep in the middle of the night by the whole of my bed juddering. It was the same sort of buzzing sensation that I had felt on my nipple but on a much larger scale. A few minutes later it all stopped and I settled back down to sleep. It was to be five days later when it happened again and this time I did acknowledge that Spirit were in fact trying very hard to tell me something, but what?

My answer to this question was a simple one. I needed to follow my heart where work was concerned and that way things would go the way my pathway intended more quickly. You see the buzzing was around my heart area. Then it happened to my whole body whilst I was asleep saying that I should take notice of my sleeping hours and therefore my dream state. As soon as I did this all the ideas for this book and much more came to fruition. It was as if Spirit could not get my attention to tell me things for me personally because I was too busy linking with and to them, for other people. You will find that all Mediums are guilty of this one. So they gave sensations that they knew I would not only take notice of but knew I would be able to understand the meaning once I gave the subject my full attention.

At another book store, where I was demonstrating and signing books, and there had been a mix up about us coming and we had not got a lot of space. There was a large table placed diagonally in front of me and a chair with ski type legs placed behind the table so that there was a book shelf diagonally situated behind me leaving a small gap where we could get through to the chair by the side shelf. We placed our briefcase, camera, handbags, etc onto an empty part of the bookshelf at my right hand side.

We decided that the space was a little tight to place the other chair next to mine so left it out. I had finished my first demonstration of the day and was busy talking to two ladies who were at the start of the queue of people waiting to speak to me and get their books signed I became aware that My Guardian Angel, Mr R had stepped up really close behind my right hand side Making me feel freezing cold but was busy so didn't take any notice.

A minute later, the lady at the front of the queue said "my God Jean is your Guardian Angel that you were just talking about here, because I am freezing cold?" This created a response from all the people in the queue, "Yes it has suddenly gone icy cold." I replied "Yes he is here but I do not understand why he is coming so close at this moment in time because this usually means that he is letting me know that he is protecting me from something"

The lady at the front responded with: "Well I am not going to cause you any harm, I can assure you that you are safe with me!" I laughed and assured her that I knew this, before I quickly turned to check with Mr R why he was worried? As I did so I noticed a young teenage couple manoeuvring towards the handbags etc.

I asked Chris to squeeze a chair in, between me and the shelf and although it was a tight squeeze, she managed it. It then warmed up and I looked round to find that the young couple had gone. Mr R was purely trying to warn me that my belongings were unsafe.

One morning as I set about my daily business I became aware of a little white Westie dog in Spirit who was following me about. I want you to remember at this point that dogs communicate from the Spirit World in the same way as they did whilst alive on the earth.

In other words they do not suddenly develop the ability to talk. Not in my experience anyway. I believe that this is because animals are extremely evolved Spirits, more evolved than humans are. So much so that they communicate by using the love vibration that is the link to life here as we know it and life after death.

This little dog followed me about for several days and I asked Mr R if he could tell me who he belonged to? He answered: "You will find out soon my child. It is close to you." I racked my brains to try and remember where there was a little Westie dog connected to someone close but this was to no avail, so I gave up trying to work it out and decided to wait until Spirit were ready to show me.

Approximately two weeks after this little dogs first appearance, I was talking to a lady and her Grandmother told me that she was very happy in her life but the last week her whole family had been touched with sadness. She immediately replied "Yes our little Terrier dog has just died after fourteen years." I replied "He wasn't white by any chance was he?" She answered without hesitation "No he was brown,"

Do you remember, that my catch phrase is: 'Do not think whilst you link.' Well on this occasion I had just broken my own rule and thought about the little white dog that had been following me in the hopes of communicating with someone whom I could give a message to. I was annoyed with myself but hey, I am human too aren't I?

At that point a little brown terrier came running up and Mr R made me aware that the dog had severe arthritis in his leg because of an old injury, and that he had a deformity type lump on his leg too. I repeated this to the lady and she said, "yes he broke a leg when he was a puppy and arthritis had set in as he got older." She then asked which leg and who can blame her for being suspicious after the error I had just made?

Remember she had never met me before. I immediately retorted well it was the right side, the broken leg was the back leg but the deformity lump was on the front leg on the same side and it itched and irritated her immensely and she kept scratching it. A beaming smile came to her face and she said, "that is right." The lump was from a tic bite that had become infected and she would not leave it alone. I am so glad she is okay. Now because of the accuracy of the most recent information she knew that her dog was there.

All is well that ends well as you would say but a little thought about not thinking always comes in handy. I could ask Spirit and prove that the dog was present but when you are first training you cannot always do this. Although I have to be honest I think this was meant to take place to plant a seed in this lady's mind so that she would not always listen to the first input on any given information because it is not always as straight forward as that.

For my part, I was not meant to be linking at that moment in time but going about my daily business which required thought. The two things combined led me to think whilst I linked, a no, no in accurate Spirit Linking and as I have just pointed out, can lead to mistakes where the information that is being given is concerned.

Later that day I visited my daughter Dawn and as we were having a cup of coffee she suddenly shuddered and asked who was standing to the left of her because she could feel the cold air moving backward and forward. I told her not to worry because it was my Dad, her Grandfather. I said he is bringing you laughter and support. She suddenly jigged up and down excitedly whilst shuddering as she said:

"Mum he has just blown on my neck."

We all laughed as I assured her that it was in fun and she asked me if I knew what Spirit animal was around her home lately, because she could hear a small animal jumping off the bed, and could also feel one brush against her legs.

It was at this point, the little white Westie who had been around me for the last two weeks came running into the room and rubbed up against her leg and she retorted:

"Mum it has just done it again."

So I asked her if she was connected to anyone who had previously owned a white Westie type dog. Her immediate response was "yes" it was the relative of someone from her past who had owned the dog so she therefore knew it very well at that time, but asked why it would choose to come through to her now? The answer was and is a simple one.

The dog is now in Spirit, and its owner who got on really well with

Dawn has recently passed too. Because our two families are no longer connected he sent the dog along first to test the; water so to speak, to see if he would be a welcome visitor, which of course he was. So you see, Mr R was right again, wasn't he?

Chapter Three
Reflections

3

Reflections

A question that people frequently ask me is: How do I know when someone whom I am talking to could develop to become a Medium? The answer is an exceptionally easy one because the answer is all in the eyes. Our eyes are the windows to our soul which means that if you look into someone's eyes, they reflect the real them. Spirit uses our eyes and our soul to be able to communicate with us. We have a reflective part of our brain on the right hand side that works almost like a mirror.

Spirit step up close within our Auric field, (which is magnetic) and use their psychic energy (which is just like static electricity as I have already stated) to reflect a shadow of their image through our eyes by touching our soul and using the reflective part of our brain to mirror image themselves. To the trained eye it is easy to spot the light and reflections in that person's eyes whilst this is taking place. People constantly remark on a person's eyes if they have the ability to link with the Spirit World. I should know because it has been the story of my life.

Whilst asleep we are on the same vibration as Spirit so therefore become part of their World. We all know that if we are asleep in a room whilst people in that room are talking, we cannot hear the conversation that is taking place. It is in fact as if we are not there at all. Does this ring a bell within your thoughts? Spirit sometimes move close to those same people when they are talking in the room where you are sleeping yet it is as if they are not there at all because they are on a different vibration, just like you whilst you are asleep. Those same Spirit visitors are however, on the same vibration as you during sleep which allows them to hold a conversation with you. They do this by using the reflective part of your brain because your brain is active whilst in sleep state. The Spirit who is communicating with you simply throws a reflection of themselves through to your eyes when using this reflective part of your brain which in turn shows pictures similar to a film at the cinema, but using the back of your eyelids as a screen. I believe that when rapid eye movement takes place during sleep state, we are trying to make sense of all the pictures that we are being shown at the back of our eyelids, meaning that we are constantly looking everywhere to take in the whole story. This is the part where our brain which is seeing these pictures back to front and upside down turns them into story form and in that process they become jumbled.

Once you realise and accept that you are communicating with the Spirit World whilst asleep, you are one step closer to linking with them whilst you are awake. This is where my dream analysis exercises starting in the next chapter come into play. As soon as a person becomes aware of the fact that they can link and communicate with those in the Spirit World on a very high Spiritual level, everything around and about that person changes. Just as love changes everything so does knowing we have the ability to link with Spirit. This is because Spirit exist on the vibration of love and this helps the real us to shine through. Before the realisation hit me that the people with whom I had communicated easily all my life were in fact dead people, I used to let people take advantage of my good nature because the Spiritual part of my soul was aware that the way to go forward was by sending out only kindness and not retaliating when people did unkind or unjust things. However, once I took the transition into a Spiritual life and daily communicated with those in the Spirit World who could guide me in the right direction, my life changed. There were a whole lot of changes which at first seemed to be a difficult comparison to my life before this.

One of the most difficult things for me to get used to was the fact that if you watch the reflections in someone's eyes, you can tell straight away if they are telling lies. This is because if someone is lying to us then this shows in the eyes too because the light reflection in our eyes is different due to the fact that the part of us that is Spirit shines through and just as we attempt to drop our eyes as if in shame because we are lying our Spirit reflects downwards which creates a dull shadow in our eyes. So you see you can learn how to read in someone's eyes if they are lying to you. This is the reason that my Father told me when I was a young child not to trust anyone who would not look me in the eye.

The reason that it is difficult being able to tell if someone is lying to you is because if you are genuinely on a Spiritual path, you need to keep the fact that you have spotted this to yourself but act accordingly to protect your own pathway. I know that thoughts are probably going through your head as you are reading this that the next time you divert away from the truth you will not look the person in the eye who you are talking to. Unfortunately or fortunately, whichever way you choose to look at it, it doesn't work that way because when Spirit use their psychic energy to touch our soul it causes a juddering sensation within the Aura. That juddering can easily be spotted by the trained eye even when the person telling untruths is on the telephone, it causes a stutter type vibration in that person's voice when added to the static on the telephone line.

So you see it is never easy to get away with not telling the truth to a well trained Medium. But you should never trust a person who will not look you in the eye whilst they are talking to you anyway. My Father is definitely right about that. The main reason that this is so difficult is because it is very hard not to react differently with someone whom you know is not being honest with you or running you or someone else whom you love down, behind your back. People soon learn when they know me well that just because I do not mention that I know something it does not necessarily mean that I do not know about it. I am told that I have a unique way of letting slip the fact that I do know things, without causing unnecessary offence or distress, but definitely putting the point across when the time is right.

The only way that you can work out what this would feel like without training the ability to do it, is by imagining what it would be like to know that something either exciting or devastating is about to occur in your life, and someone has let slip to you what is going to happen, and asked you to promise that you will not let on that you know!!!

For instance they tell you that your daughter is pregnant but keeping it a secret from you and you are hurt by this because you thought that she would tell you first. Can you imagine what that would feel like? You would have to keep your promise and keep quiet about it but every time your daughter spoke to you, you would feel that your relationship was a lie.

We are here to learn certain lessons and the first and hardest lesson to learn when you are a placid and/or Spiritual person, is to love yourself. I used to believe that loving yourself was a selfish and egotistical thing to do, but I was wrong. We each have a pathway in life that will make the most of our assets.

Every living soul has good things within their character and make up. We need to extend the use of these talents to take us forward on our lifetime pathway. If, however, we choose to let people treat us unjustly, this will slow down our life cycle by altering the energies around us to negative ones, whereas if we learn to say no on these occasions without becoming aggressive, then the energies around us will become more and more positive which will bring good in our direction, so keeping us on our pathway. If asked to help people, I used to always say yes even if it was to my detriment, whereas now I have learnt to say, "sorry I have not got the time at the moment so cannot help you this time."

By doing this I have moved a lot further on my lifetime Spiritual path which in effect has enabled me to meet and help more people. You do however need to be aware that those people who were just using you will back away and stop involving you in things. This may hurt but it allows you to face the truth and in doing so it stops these people from altering your pathway to a different direction. The trick is, never to act upon anything that you hear through the third person. This is because jealousy and envy are very strong emotions which in the hands of an egotistical and manipulative person can come out as lies in their attempt to spoil things for the person/people they are jealous of or in fact trying to control.

My belief in life is that if someone tells me something bad about someone whom I connect with, I listen if I must then say "well until I see for myself that this person is behaving badly towards me, it is not my problem." You also need to be aware that these people always try to make sure that the person they are manipulating never speaks to the person they are telling lies about. In this way it takes longer for the truth to come out, and they are in control of the damaging situation that they have created.

Remember that on death we receive compensation and retribution for all good and bad deeds here on the earth. Therefore, it is a good idea to forgive the person who is wronging you and surround them in good wishes. This way they give retribution for what they have done to all involved in the above situation and you do not get dragged into their downward spiral and have to give retribution too.

Thoughts are living things. We should therefore be aware that our thoughts travel, not only to the Spirit World but to the person whom the thoughts are about or for? In other words, when we start to think about someone, we automatically come in to that person's head, because thoughts are living things and as such reach out to the destination to which they are intended? This is so whether those thoughts are good or bad? We should therefore try to never think bad thoughts about anyone, and only wish them well whilst thinking about them. It is after all often said that as people, we should forgive and forget things that are done against us. I always forgive people if they have upset or hurt me in any way. But I have to admit that I believe that it is impossible to forget any bad deeds.

This is why when I say forgive, I am not asking you to forget because this is impossible, when our brain has a storage mechanism enabling us to remember things that take place in our life. We remember traumatic things or really happy occasions with more ease than the mundane things in life.

Our memory is, do you agree, a very large part of who we are? For instance, if a baby touches a fire and burns a finger, they remember not to touch it in future, as it will hurt them. If they forgot this lesson then they would be in constant danger of hurting themselves, giving a very good and plausible reason why I believe that we are meant to remember, because this is how we learn our lessons. For instance, when at school we are taught to write which gives us the tools and ability to further ourselves on our life's path, we did not start off with the ability because it was a memory; we needed to learn for ourselves in order to follow our ordained pathway in life. If we were given the knowledge at birth there would be no way of knowing if we knew what we needed to go forward and if we forgot we would have to learn this skill all over again, just like some unfortunate people have to do after a serious accident or illness where their memory is erased.

The same reason for remembering has to be said for people who hurt us, in some way. Our memory of that pain teaches us to be careful in future. This in turn strengthens our character, and makes us less susceptible to being taken for granted. Unfortunately, it can also work in reverse, because sometimes we react towards people in a way that is unfair because we have been hurt by someone else in the past. Some people deliberately pull away from someone who loves them, and they love in return, just in case they are going to get hurt. When really they would not have been hurt, but have created "cause and effect" and made the very thing that they were afraid of, happen.

In other words they would rather walk away from the friendship or relationship, than risk being hurt by that person walking away from them. In effect, by doing this, they are in fact hurting themselves and the other person who has been good to them and has no intention of ever walking away. This is cause and effect. However, the person who walks away needs to remember that this person will always be alive in their thoughts, this is also so in reverse. Meaning those two people will always miss one another from time to time because both of those people's destinies have been changed by them backing away unnecessarily.

The same is so when someone passes to Spirit. Because we did not really want them to leave, they remain in our memories, ready to reappear from time to time. Although in this case the dead person was meant to depart, the living person was just not ready to see them go.

True love can cross great distances, thereby reuniting two people together, even when they have not physically connected to each other, either by sight or verbally for some time. This means that if you are in trouble emotionally or physically, and you think strongly about the person that you need support from, then that help will eventually arrive. This is so, whether that person is still in the land of the living, or in the Spirit world. Sometimes these things take longer than we expect because people can be strong willed and Spirit need time to set the wheels in motion for changes to occur. However, there is no way of stopping events from taking place when loving thoughts are sent out because we are then linking two people here on earth and a person or people in the Spirit world, to make the goodness take place. Therefore, love links two people eternally no matter how far the distance between them.

Not even death can separate two people who love one another, because their love is kept alive by thoughts, and thoughts are living things that can travel the distance no matter how far. So remember, if you no longer see or associate with someone whom you love, then every time that you send them a thought, your love will put something good into their life. This can, and will travel the distance between two living souls, or the dead and the living. Because of this fact, it is important never to allow the fact that you are upset by someone's actions, to encourage you to think badly of that person.

They did after all feel that they were justified in their actions. But if they were wrong then they need your love more than ever. Love is the 'Light Of Vibration Eternity' and as such can fill voids and reunite souls both here and on the Spirit side of life.

Help to make someone else's life run smoothly by sending them as much love as you can. This cannot and will not stop bad things from happening to that person if these things are meant to be. But, it will give them the strength they need to fight their way back through to good and happy times. If you think about it, if we forget that someone has wronged us and we are kind to that person, it is not that we have learned the lesson not to take on board their problems and wish them well anyway, but simply because we do not remember being wronged by them. However, if we remember but are nice to them anyway whilst not allowing their problem to spoil, slow down or even stop us doing what our life pathway has ordained us to do; we have then learned this lesson and can move forward. I am pointing all this out to you so that you will be aware that your Soul/Spirit belongs to you and you are the only one who has responsibility for it. Do not take on board other people's problems as your own, even when trying to help them. Love yourself first and then spread all the love that you have drawn into your being to those who need your help. If you do it this way, it will really work because, like attracts like, and Love is the Light Of Vibration Eternity. Without placing this love within your Aura by loving yourself, how can you possibly bring love to others and help them onto their right pathway?

If you relax and try, it is always possible to feel the love that emanates from the Spirit World because Love is anything that you feel comfortable with in your heart, therefore all you need to do is trust that they are there and will not hurt you, and that love will show itself within your whole being, which in turn will enable you to feel the love that emanates from the Spirit World.

We are travelling through a very Spiritual age at this moment in time, and it is therefore the time when everyone can become aware of the changing energies around us. This is the right time for us all to unite in the love which is the light of vibration eternity, to try to unite the earth with love. The world at this time is like a twisting kaleidoscope full of all the colours in the rainbow moving us all in turn with the earth's rhythms. If we pull together, those rhythms will be vibrations of love, and therefore link us to and with the World of Spirit. Spirit visitors have a tendency to come visiting in pairs when they want to communicate with animals and babies. They do this with one standing to the left and the other to the right. This encourages the one being visited to use their peripheral vision by using their eyes separately, with the right eye looking to the right and the left eye looking to the left. This creates the conditions for two things which are:

1) The stimulation of their third eye which in turn will allow them to start to see extra worldly things besides those that are considered to be naturally around them.

2) As they stare at their new found source of interest in their vision, they become aware of the vibrational changes that are around them. This allows them to see and be aware of the Spirit visitors that may be invisible to others situated in the same vicinity as where the animals or babies are. They then get excited by what they are seeing and sensing because the vibrational changes make them feel excited which in turn helps them to see the Spirit visitors more clearly, Animals and babies are generally known to see spirit.

I feel that this is purely because they are excited by things quicker than adults are, so therefore change the vibrations around them naturally without trying, whereas adults tend to try too hard, which tends to have the opposite effect and serves to lower their vibrations instead; thereby taking them further away from the Spirit visitors.

I was lying in bed one Friday night talking to the Spirit World because I could not sleep as is usual for me, when I noticed a Spirit Yorkshire Terrier near to my bed. As I watched the dog intently she suddenly walked straight through the bedroom wall into the next door house. Now as I have said before, there is nothing wrong with that because it is very easy for Spirit to go through anything because of the fact that everything is made up of molecules and can easily be dematerialised or broken down and re-materialised or replaced whole at the moment of passing through anything. But the thing that I found strange was that although I knew that my next door neighbour had two Yorkshire terrier dogs, I was not aware that either of them had died, yet here she was giving a message for her owner. The following morning as I went out to my car, my next door neighbour called me over and said that one of her little Yorkies had needed to be put to sleep because she was very poorly and she wondered whether she had got home safe to the Spirit side of life? I immediately asked her if she had died the previous night to which she responded "no' she died on Thursday evening". This really surprised me and I explained to her what had happened the previous night, (which was Friday and not Thursday) and explained that normally a dog would do that on the night they died in order to pass on a message to their owner that they were home safe and okay. I asked if anything had happened to do with the dog the previous evening. She immediately replied with a huge smile on her face "My partner fetched her home from the Vets where she was put to sleep and we buried her in the garden last night (Friday). Now it all made sense, she was asking me to let her family know that she had indeed arrived home safe and had come to spend some time with them from the Spirit side of life that evening. This bought a smile to her owners face. So you see even animals can give a message from the Spirit World. No they cannot talk to us, they are just as they were here but if you listen to what they are not saying like I did when this little dog went through my wall, they can say a lot just as we can.

Chapter Four
Time to Practice

4
Time to Practice

You will need a few tools before you start and these tools are very simple and not that costly. They are:

A notebook.

A pen or pencil.

A pack of Jean Kelford Dream step Cards.

My cards will be available from most book shops, where you bought this book or from my web sites, which you will find details of, in the back of the book.

Now you are ready to begin. I would ask that you keep the above tools next to your bedside so that they are ready at hand because the first parts of development are very easy if you have this equipment close to where you sleep. Here are some easy to follow exercises in order to get used to your dream step cards and what you can do with them. The ways with which you can use these cards come in many forms and are almost limitless. Here is a very simple exercise to practice whilst awake that has nothing to do with analysing dreams, it is just to start you off on your pathway to dream analysis. Everyone has a name, even if it is one that we choose for ourselves. We are going to use that name by using the art of numerology to help you to create your own reading. All you have to do is follow these very simple steps but using your name instead of mine. My name is: JEAN. Therefore the numbers that coincide with my name are ditto:

J = 10
E = 05

A = 01
N =14

This is because J is the tenth letter in the alphabet; E is the fifth letter etc. So you see it is a very easy principle to follow. Write your first name down as I have written mine with the number that it coincides with written next to it. I have written down this chart with each letter of the alphabet and the number that they represent to help you with this. Take the cards out of your pack that fit with the letters of your name. If it starts with:

A = 01- example:	A is for ANNETTE	1st card out of the pack.
B – 02- example:	B is for BURT	2nd card out of the pack.
C = 03- example:	C is for CHRISTINE	3rd card out of the pack.
D = 04- example:	D is for DEAN	4th card out of the pack.
E = 05- example:	E is for ETHEL	5th card out of the pack.
F = 06- example:	F is for FREDRICK	6th card out of the pack.
G = 07- example:	G is for GEMMA	7th card out of the pack.
H = 08- example:	H is for HARRY	8th card out of the pack.
I = 09- example:	I is for ISOBEL	9th card out of the pack.
J = 10- example:	J is for JAMES	10th card out of the pack.
K = 11- example:	K is for KAREN	11th card out of the pack.
L = 12- example:	L is for LEN	12th card out of the pack.
M = 13- example:	M is for MERVYN	13th card out of the pack.

N = 14- example: N is for NELLY   14th card out of the pack.

O = 15- example: O is for OSCAR   15th card out of the pack.

P = 16- example: P is for PAMELA   16th card out of the pack.

Q = 17- example: Q is for QUENTIN   17th card out of the pack.

R = 18- example: R is for ROBIN   18th card out of the pack.

S = 19- example: S is for SCOTT   19th card out of the pack.

T = 20- example: T is for TONI   20th card out of the pack.

W = 21- example: W is for William   21st card out of the pack.

V = 22- example: V is for VERA   22nd card out of the pack.

U = 23- example: U is for UNA   23rd card out of the pack.

X = 24- example: X is for XYON   24th card out of the pack.

Y = 25- example: Y is for YAN   25th card out of the pack.

Z = 26- example: Z is for ZOE   26th card out of the pack.

Now take each card and place them out in front of you in the order that your name dictates them to be, going down in a line.

The cards for my name would be:

Card 10:
DREAM VIBRATIONS.

Your dream vibrations are bringing a loved one in Spirit close to you right now.

Think of the person whom you most want to hear from in the Spirit World before you go to sleep for three concurrent nights. That person will appear in your dreams and Guide you forward in life.

Card 5:
BLUE LIGHT.

It is time to communicate with your own Spirit and your Guardian Angel.

You know in your heart of hearts what is right for you because your Spirit is telling you, but sometimes we need added help and this is where the blue light for communication comes in. Listen to what people are saying around you, and if the same thing is repeated three times, this will help your dreams come true.

Card 1:
ABILITY.

Like everything else in this world of ours, the more ability you have the further you can go. All you have to do is develop ability that believe it or not you were born with.

By developing the ability you have at your disposal you will reach the heights you deserve. So now is the time to go for it. Reach for the skies.

Card 14:
FINANCIAL REWARDS.

You now reap what you have sown financially.

If you have worked hard, or been well behaved you will now reap your financial rewards, however, if you have been resting on your laurels where work or behaviour is concerned, expect a big disappointment right now.

Now, take the sentence from the top of each card just under the title and place them together in order. Adding an occasional word between the writing on each card in capital letters as below making the reading flow in story form out of the words on your cards, as mine do below:

Your dream vibrations are bringing a loved one in Spirit close to you right now. Because it is time to communicate with your own Spirit and your Guardian Angel. REMEMBER like everything else in this world of ours, the more ability you have the further you can go. All you have to do is develop ability that believe it or not you were born with; defining that you now reap what you have sown financially.

Now do the same thing with the writing at the bottom of the card to get a better understanding of what you are being told.

Think of the person whom you most want to hear from in the Spirit World before you go to sleep for three concurrent nights. That person will appear in your dreams and Guide you forward in life. You know in your heart of hearts what is right for you because your Spirit is telling you, but sometimes we need added help and this is where the blue light for communication comes in. Listen to what people are saying around you and if the same thing is repeated three times this will help your dreams come true. All you have to do is develop the ability you have at your disposal and you will reach the heights you deserve. So now is the time to go for it. Reach for the skies!

When you read between the lines in this reading it is telling me that I am to think of the Spirit world before sleeping which anyone who knows me and has been to any of my workshops will tell you, that I not only do this but I advise others to do it too. It talks about me knowing deep down what is right for me because of my Spirit communicating to me through the blue light of communication which is and always has been part of my everyday life. It tells me to develop the ability which I have done and it also says that I will draw towards what I have earned. This has been my belief for a long time. So you see the reading from my name says a lot about who I am and the same can be said for everyone.

Let's take this exercise a little further and use my cards to see what our initials tell us. I should make it clear that I wrote the cards before the exercises and not the other way round. My Initials of my first name and my surname are JK which works out at:

J = 10
K= 11

Here are the cards:

Card 10:
DREAM VIBRATIONS

Your dream vibrations are bringing a loved one in Spirit close to you right now.

Think of the person whom you most want to hear from in the Spirit World before you go to sleep for three concurrent nights. That person will appear in your dreams and Guide you forward in life.

Card 11:
EXPECT THE BEST

You will receive what you expect to receive right now so expect the best.

The energies around you at this moment are exceptionally good but you will only get what you expect, so make the effort to expect the best and the effort will be made for the best to occur.

When put together they say:

Your dream vibrations are bringing a loved one in Spirit close to you right now. You will receive what you expect to receive right now so expect the best.

And the more in-depth version is:

Think of the person whom you most want to hear from in the Spirit World before you go to sleep for three concurrent nights. That person will appear in your dreams and Guide you forward in life. The energies around you at this moment are exceptionally good but you will only get what you expect, so make the effort to expect the best and the effort will be made for the best to occur.

Once again I am being reminded about Spirit being able to Guide me, and I am being told to look out for the good things to happen because I will get what I expect. At this point it is a good idea to add your middle name initial to the equation to see if it alters your prospects at all? My middle name initial is: V

$V = 22$

Here is the appropriate card:

Card 22:
IT IS NOT THE RIGHT TIME

Do not hurry the situation just now because the time is not yet right for you.

It is your time to relax with the situation around you at this moment because it will all go wrong if you try to hurry things whereas, if you wait, your time will come and all will be yours.

This is how it changes the reading:

Your dream vibrations are bringing a loved one in Spirit close to you right now. You will receive what you expect to receive right now so expect the best. But do not hurry the situation just now because the time is not yet right for you.

With the in-depth version saying:

Think of the person whom you most want to hear from in the Spirit World before you go to sleep for three concurrent nights. That person will appear in your dreams and Guide you forward in life. The energies around you at this moment are exceptionally good but you will only get what you expect, so make the effort to expect the best and the effort will be made for the best to occur. It is your time to relax with the situation around you at this moment because it will all go wrong if you try to hurry things whereas, if you wait, your time will come and all will be yours.

The finished reading from my initials says:

Once again I am being reminded about Spirit being able to Guide me, and I am being told to look out for the good things to happen because I will get what I expect but not to try to hurry them because the time has to be right for whatever I am doing in life.

Can you see how it works that if you have not got all the details you may inadvertently change events thereby altering your destiny? This is the reason why it is not a good idea to tell a person about someone that they are about to meet and get involved with unless you have the whole story. If you read through the reading for JK and then read it again when V is added I am sure that you will agree that your actions would differ slightly once you are in possession of all the information and not just some of it. I think that you will find it interesting to see the end results if I use my two former surnames which are my maiden name and my first married name.

C was my maiden name which made my initials JVC.

C = 3
Here is the card:

Card 3:
BIRTH.

You have drawn the birth card because new beginnings are being offered in your life right now.

New beginnings are yours for the taking so be brave and your life will take definite swings for the better. This card indicates a new and better life for you right now.

Here are the changed end readings:

Your dream vibrations are bringing a loved one in Spirit close to you right now. Do not hurry the situation just now because the time is not yet right for you. You have drawn the birth card because new beginnings are being offered in your life right now.

Here is the in-depth version:

Think of the person whom you most want to hear from in the Spirit World before you go to sleep for three concurrent nights. That person will appear in your dreams and Guide you forward in life. It is your time to relax with the situation around you at this moment because it will all go wrong if you try to hurry things whereas, if you wait, your time will come and all will be yours. You have drawn the birth card because new beginnings are being offered in your life right now. They are yours for the taking so be brave and your life will take definite swings for the better. This card indicates a new and better life for you.

Summed up it means:

It is telling me that I was born to communicate with Spirit and to do well in life because I was born with that but it is important and necessary for me to be brave and wait for the time to be right to make my move.

My first married initial was R. making my initials JVR

R = 18
Here is the card that coincides with the number eighteen

Card 18:
GRACE

Grace and serenity will take over your heart.

Things in your life at this minute can appear to be a bit heavy and a bit of a burden. Drawing the Grace card, means that serenity will take over your heart and mind if you let it because Spirit will grace your dreams with their presence, thereby giving you the peace of mind to go forward.

Here are the final readings for those initials:

Your dream vibrations are bringing a loved one in Spirit close to you right now. Do not hurry the situation just now because the time is not yet right for you. Serenity will take over your heart.

Think of the person whom you most want to hear from in the Spirit World before you go to sleep for three concurrent nights. That person will appear in your dreams and Guide you forward in life. It is your time to relax with the situation around you at this moment because it will all go wrong if you try to hurry things whereas, if you wait, your time will come and all will be yours. Things in your life at this minute can appear to be a bit heavy and a bit of a burden. Drawing the Grace card, means that serenity will take over your heart and mind if you let it because Spirit will grace your dreams with their presence, thereby giving you the peace of mind to go forward.

Now the story has changed with my name change it is telling me:

That I should listen to and communicate with Spirit and relax as much as I can with the situation that is a burden around me because peace of mind and heart are on the way to allow me to go forward.

When you work it out this is how the story has spanned out for me so far:

My birth story is:

It is telling me that I was born to communicate with Spirit and to do well in life because I was born with that gift but it is important and necessary for me to be brave and wait for the time to be right to make my move.

It changed with my first marriage into:

That I should listen to and communicate with Spirit and relax as much as I can with the situation that is a burden around me because peace of mind and heart are on the way to allow me to go forward.

Then with my second marriage, which is the stage of my life where I am now, it is:

Once again I am being reminded about Spirit being able to Guide me, and I am being told to look out for the good things to happen because I will get what I expect but not to try to hurry them because the time has to be right for whatever I am doing in life to go well.

I know that this may seem a long drawn out process to follow but when you are doing it personally for your own initials, you will be surprised at how quick it will come together and you will be looking towards the next exercise and the next stage of your development.

Chapter Five

Coincidences or Not?

5
Coincidences or not?

It is very interesting when we take the time to look at some instances in life when it appears that coincidences are taking place. But as I have already said, I do not believe in coincidence, so thought that I would include a few to see what you make of it.

My Father, whose name was Mervyn, I am more or less certain knew nothing about numerology and things like that, so I know that he did not choose his lucky number in that way any more than I did mine. His lucky number was thirteen which he told me many times and thought that it was a little strange that most people had a problem with the number thirteen because of superstition, when for him it had always had lucky connotations. If we look at my alphabet chart we find that M is number thirteen, therefore his first name starts with his lucky number. It was a number that always seemed to work for him and bought him luck. I must admit that it has never been a problem for me either.

Card M reads:
FAITH.

Life is what you make it. Have the faith to trust and make changes.

In order for you to come out on top in your present situation, you need to have faith in yourself and all those connected to you. If you have faith you will win the day.

Strange as it may seem, this was definitely my Dad's philosophy in life as I am sure it is in death. My Father taught me a lot and holding your head up high, whilst taking a chance to go for what you want was one of them. I can remember him saying to me when I was a young girl: "Bean you make your own luck in this life. For me luck comes in a "bakers dozen," I learned that when I was a lad at the bakery. Obviously by this comment, I am sure that you realise that my Father had worked at a bakery as a young boy. Just as a matter of interest I was born in the house that my Mum still lives in, which although it is number fifteen, it should have been number thirteen. My Father and Mother did not choose the house as such, it was offered to them, so is this a coincidence or not?

One of my lucky numbers has always been number twenty two. I used to think that it was because I was born on the twenty second but now I think that maybe it is the other way round and I was born on that date because it was my lucky number. Or is that just another coincidence!! Remember my middle name starts with the letter that coincides with number twenty two as well. I thought that my readers would be interested to hear that the day after I wrote the above, it was my birthday and as I got up in the morning I saw my Dad who is in Spirit. He looked at me and said: "Bean, when you are made aware of thirteen, something good will happen it is a present from your old dad. Remember it is lucky" After saying this he promptly smiled and disappeared. I should tell you that Bean was my Dad's nickname for me. I smiled because it is always good to see my Dad let alone on my birthday but could not help but wonder what he had meant by his statement!!!

After rising from bed, dressing and eating my breakfast, I settled down to open my cards and presents. After doing this I decided to count my birthday cards even though I knew that I would be receiving more later on in the day. To my surprise there were thirteen cards and what my Dad had said that morning immediately came to mind. I explained to Mike and he just smiled. He is used to me and my surprise messages from the Spirit World that always manage to come true even when they look unlikely. We forgot about it for the time being and got on with our day. However, about thirty minutes later I told Mike that I was going to book our car in for an MOT because it would be three years old the following month and we were going to change it for a new one. Just as I picked up the telephone he asked: "Jean why don't we go to the garage and look at and order the new car instead, and we can book the MOT whilst we are there?" I immediately indicated that this would be a really good idea and we set off to the garage.

We decided to look at the cars first and order one for the end of September, which would coincide with our car's third birthday. Once we had decided which car we were having we spoke to the sales representative who worked out that he could arrange it so that if we had the new car at the beginning of September instead of the end we would not have to have the major service done or the MOT on our present car because our car would go in part exchange and he could also give us over £700 saving on the car, which meant that we saved approximately £1000 in all by going car shopping that day. My immediate thought was 'Thanks Dad that is a fantastic birthday present.' Just to end a happy story I counted my cards again later that day after receiving more and discovered that there were now twenty two cards. One of my lucky numbers connected to my name. Coincidence or not!!! I know my opinion, what is yours? If we use the principle of numerology and add together our letters and numbers, what do we get? My name numbers and letters when I was born were:

J = 10
V= 22
C = 03

Adding them together = 10 + 22 + 03 = 35   --- 03 + 05 = 8
By coincidence, or not! Seven and eight have always been lucky numbers for me too. When I was married the first time my initials became:

J = 10
V = 22
R = 18

Adding them together = 10 + 22 + 18 = 50 ----- 5 + 0 = 5

Five has never meant anything at all to me. When I remarried my initials became:

J = 10
V = 22
K = 11

Adding them together = 10 + 22 + 11 = 43   ----- 04 + 03 = 7

Seven again!! Remember it has always been a lucky number for me. This maybe tells me that my first marriage was not for me. My card reading stated that there were burdens in my life during the time when five was the prominent number in my life. I remember being told by someone at that phase in my life that I should change my name because maybe the numerology of my name was drawing bad things towards me. At the time I was not sure that this could make any difference at all but thanked her anyway and said that I would remember it. I think that it is important to say here that by changing your name, this does not mean divorce your partner unless of course you have got good reason to do so. Now that Spirit has indicated more information about this subject to me, I realise that really it is not that the numerology of your name draws bad to you but in fact the other way round. Influences are made to draw these things to us because our life's lessons dictate the need for a learning curve in that direction. I believe that this is the reason why sometimes people use a hyphenated name or even keep their maiden name even though they are married instead of taking on the partner's surname, even though the person probably did not realise it at the time. I do not think that the same principle counts if you check the numerology and change or not change your name because of it unless you also change the life pattern that is causing your problems. Remember at this point we are attracted to the person whom we marry or are going to become friends with for reasons that are sometimes out of our control. With my first marriage I was picking up on serious doubts and trying to postpone the wedding, but allowed myself to worry about others feelings instead of my own life and where it should be leading. I should have listened to my own Spirit because I was being pre-warned about possible repercussions and alterations to my life's pathway. I ignored this hence the burdens causing stumbling blocks that we talked about earlier.

We should actually stop and think about our future actions and how they would not only affect the life of others but our own life. Remember if nothing is coincidence, then it must be created by cause and effect. Each action you take in this life has a ripple effect so that the lives and therefore the pathways of the people around you are affected, maybe in small things or sometimes in really big ways. The reason I am telling you this is because if you look back to my reason for getting married when I did, instead of postponing, allowing us to work things out better, it was because I was worried about the effect on other people. Sadly by going ahead simply to protect them, the ripple effect for them and others lead me to have worse repercussions. This means that instead of helping them in the way I thought I was doing I changed their life too. I would like you to remember at this point that we have personal responsibility for our own lives, not for anyone else's, so it is a good idea to look after your life and allow others to do the same, unless of course the other person is too young, too old or infirm and cannot take responsibility for their own life anymore. If this is the case then it is important to do what is necessary to make sure that they are safe, loved and looked after without becoming a martyr and giving up your hopes, dreams and in turn your life for that other person.

If this is you and your life, was it intended that you would have responsibility for another human being so that you could learn the lesson that you can look after the other person without giving up on yourself, if you really look into your options? Would you, or have you failed this common test in our World? One of the commonest things that I am told as a Medium is: "I do not deserve good because I had an abortion and I am now being punished." This definitely comes into the category of personal responsibility because although there are many good arguments against abortion because we are in effect taking a life, there are also many arguments why abortion should at times take place too. The Spirit of a person needs to touch the earth to go on in Spirit and do many things to help in this World. These people need to find parents where it is not possible for them to be here on the earth with those people, so choose to either become an abortion, miscarriage or ectopic pregnancy so that they can touch the earth but not live here on the earth as we know it.

Generally speaking this is the reason why these things take place and have nothing to do with the Mother or Father being a bad person Therefore, they are definitely not punished in that way. Any punishment that would be necessary comes from the fact that the Mother or in-deed the Father has guilt feelings sometimes for many years, which hold them back and alters their pathway. Usually these things happen after a lot of thought and deliberation. It is therefore extremely unlikely that a child who was meant to live on the earth was aborted, miscarried or lost to this earth in any other way. The parents of these children had a lesson to learn whilst travelling their pathway of life, they had choices to make and those choices defined whether they had indeed learned the lesson that was being presented to them or not. Incidentally children who go to the Spirit World in this way are allowed to choose a name for them self as soon as they are old enough to do so, unless it happens that, such as in the case of my daughter Toni, when she had a miscarriage; she had already named her much wanted son. The name she had chosen was George. The first letter of the name George falls in the alphabet as one of my lucky numbers, which again is seven. Again is this coincidence or not? This is what card seven says:

Card 7:
COMMUNICATION

Once again you need to listen to anything that is in triplicate. Spirit are trying to give help and advice at this time by letting you overhear conversations more than once in order to pass important information on to you. Listen carefully because it can come from a place or places you least expect. If you hear any communication three times or more then you should act upon it.

George's parents therefore need to be aware of any repetition on their life pathway because if they do not, it will alter their lives considerably. This is a gift of communication that their son George has left for them to thank them for allowing him to touch the earth. Therefore if they pay attention to this they will be guided through their lives on the right and lucky pathway, by way of a thank you from their Son. But once again we must remember that they still have personal responsibility and can ignore his advice just as anyone who is reading this book can ignore what is in it. Your life is your responsibility not mine or anyone else's.

We are drawn to names for our children for a reason. Have you ever noticed that quite often we hate our name that our parents chose for us when we are children, but invariably change our mind about it when we grow up? When I was a child I hated people calling me Jeannie which I could not understand them doing because it elongated my name instead of shortening it. I now do not mind this at all and realise that it is a term of endearment. I think that maybe I was already capable of picking up on the difference that my name could make to my life but did not realise it. Now that my life has reached the position on my pathway that it has, it no longer worries me because I have an inner understanding about the differences that it can and does make to me, especially now my name has changed.

Have you ever wondered why sometimes you hear of a singer, who is not doing very well at all, then their manager decides to change their name and they suddenly make it big? Is it coincidence? Or is it because they changed their name and drew different influences towards them? Maybe we should take into consideration that it may be because the ethos dictated that Spirit organise a change so that, that person can move forward because a certain lesson has been learned?

Animals and particularly dogs see the Spirit World visitors. The main reason for this is because they are automatically more trusting and yet more curious of new things and of strangers than we are, which incidentally is also a fact where babies and small children are concerned. Because of their innate ability to trust and be curious of what they can see, hear and feel all around them at any given time, they are usually able to avail themselves to the vibration where the Spirit World reside, which incidentally remember, is the vibration of love, and therefore freely open to animals, babies and young children naturally. It is, as we get older and become more suspicious, that we stop taking everything that we see, hear, and feel in a loving way, and this serves to slow down our ability to link into and onto a vibration that is of great interest to everyone, even non believers of its existence. This means that animals, babies and young children tend to concentrate on more than one thing at a time, which is an essential ability to use when linking in with the Spirit World. This in turn allows them to see, hear and sense things that many adults unfortunately cannot. For instance they not only hear the wind, but they can also see it. This again is another way for them to stretch their abilities of linking to those in the Spirit World, because they are using the natural ability that we are all born with to concentrate on two things at the same time frequently; hence altering their vibration on to the space where the Spirit World reside.

Unfortunately it is considered to be a fact that as we grow older most of us become less curious of things that are not easy for us to establish are there. This in turn trains us not to be curious enough to look in more than one direction at once, which negates the use of our third eye which is an essential tool, whilst linking to and with those in the Spirit World. Luckily for me, my Father was wise enough to teach me to question things that I did not understand and look for more than one reason for their existence. This taught me to constantly look for what people were not saying, which as I have made clear in this and my previous books is a very important and natural part of Spirit linking. For instance, when I stand on stage I am constantly looking at both sides of the room at all times, this naturally opens my third eye and allows me to use what I believe is my God given ability to see, hear, sense and more importantly understand why Spirit not only live on after death but visit us here to guide us. I believe that God has the unique ability to send to us whatever we need to help with any given situation. This sometimes means sending messages to encourage us that it is worth surrounding our World with love, peace and tranquillity so that we can be together as one after we leave this mortal life. I believe that each person and animal born is unique in their own way and that we all have at least one special gift that is God given to see us through our life and pathway here. It is a bit like knowing that any decent parent would not dream of telling their child to go and catch a bus to school without first making sure that they had the bus fare that they would need in order to ride on the bus. This is common sense because it is in a way giving them the tools to allow them to take on the job in hand, i.e., catching a bus to school. My belief tells me that it is the same when we are born onto the earth. We have at least one God given gift that we have the ability to be good at if we develop and use the tools available to us. Great musicians are born with that ability but have to train it. My ability is to link into, discover and teach a part of our natural World that we as human beings are forgetting to use because of the introduction of false stimuli like television, computers etc.

Strong Christians find it hard to understand why someone like me would be allowed to help people in this way when it is God's job to do this and God is very capable of carrying out this work. I agree with them in principle but I cannot help but think of the joke that goes something like:

'A man was on board a ship which sank and he hung on to a piece of driftwood to save himself from drowning in the sure knowledge and faith that God would save him from this terrible predicament. After a short while a small boat came along and offered to take him on board but the man said, "no thank you God will save me," and the boat went on its way. Next came along a ship but once again the man declined because he was sure that God would save him, then finally an helicopter that had been alerted by the ship came to take him on board to safety. The man still declined and unfortunately he died of the severe cold from the water. When the man went through the gates of heaven he said: God I am very disappointed because I trusted that you would save me and you let me die. God answered: "My son I sent you a small boat, a ship and a helicopter but you would not accept my help so what could I do?"

The reason that I am telling you this is because things are not always as straight forward as they may appear and who are we to say that Mediums are not born with this gift so that if someone needs God's help that cannot be reached in any other way then these amazing so called coincidences that may be God's work take place so that the person in need of help meets someone like myself just at the point when the need is there!!

Only recently, it was by coincidence!! Halloween day and I was attending Borders book store in Watford to demonstrate and talk about my latest book. My husband Mike told me that we did not need to get directions because it was straight off the motorway. I however was not sure of this so got the instructions off the route finder on the internet just in case. It turned out that it was a good job that I did because Mike had got Watford Borders mixed up with Brent Cross Borders. Once in store and talking to the public there was a couple who stopped to listen and bought a copy of both of my books after listening to what I had to say. They told us that they had had no intention of coming to Watford that day but had gone to Brent Cross Borders and the book that they were looking for was not available in that store at that time so they decided to travel down to Watford and just as they walked into the store I started to demonstrate and they stopped to listen. Was this do you think, coincidence or God having a quiet word with them so that they could meet me, buy my books and I in turn could help them?

So you see it is just possible that at times when God needs to help people whom he cannot reach in any other way he arranges for someone like me to help by using my God given gifts and abilities. Food for thought don't you think?

Being psychic and very spiritually aware can be very confusing to a young child to say the least, and this can be where a lot of misunderstandings take place. A typical instance of this happened to my Granddaughter as I was writing this chapter. She had been to a little friend's birthday party at a Wacky Warehouse and was excited but absolutely fine otherwise. By the time they arrived home it was past her normal bedtime and she went off to sleep fairly quickly, whacked out by the Wacky Warehouse as it were. My daughter Toni checked on her two children every so often and went to look at them once more just before their Dad returned home from his afternoon shift at work. Thomas was okay but Georgina looked very hot so her Mum pulled back the duvet and left the bedroom door open in an attempt to let some cool air circulate and cool her down. Ten minutes later when the children's Dad arrived home from work Toni said that she would just look at their daughter again to make sure that she was okay. However when she got upstairs she found Georgina lying on her back with her eyes open staring at the ceiling and shaking yet sweating at the same time. She at once took her downstairs and took her temperature to find it was very high so gave her something to help and kept her downstairs with them to keep an eye on things.

Although the medicine soon helped, she sat quietly on the sofa next to her Father so obviously was not feeling right. Suddenly she pushed her hand up and forward in front of her face as if she was pushing something or someone away and said "Tell her to stop touching my nose Dad, she is scaring me." Her parents immediately asked who was touching her nose and she said 'her', whilst pointing in front of her, then pointing to a photograph across the room said "her in the picture." They looked at the photograph to which she was referring and was shocked to find that it was a picture of Jenny my stepdaughter who died just over nine years earlier. We can only surmise that Jen was tweaking her nose to try and cheer her up. The interesting thing is that not only did this happen after her temperature had dropped making it less likely to be delirium, but Toni had asked my husband Mike (her step Dad) for a picture of Jenny just before Christmas the previous year so we gave her a framed photograph amongst her Christmas presents. It was now the beginning of May and Georgina had never once mentioned the lady in the frame before, even though her image had been on display since Christmas morning. When something like this takes place I would say that it is hard for anyone to doubt that those we love still take care of and show an interest in us after leaving their physical body, so therefore there must be and is 'life after death'. Even though the way Jenny presented herself gave Georgina cause to worry because she had never seen the lady in the picture before. Remember her step aunt died six years before she herself was born.

Chapter Six
Time for More Practice

6
Time for More Practice

For the next exercises in this book to help you to develop your Spiritual and psychic gifts, I would like to ask all readers who are interested in developing these gifts, no matter what stage of their development they are at, to humour me for a while and pretend that they have never even tried to link to and with our Spirit friends before. Then first of all I am going to suggest an exercise that simply needs for it to be after dark and for you to have four candles and somewhere to sit comfortably where you will not be disturbed. The only reasons that the darkness is necessary is because the infra red part of our eyes works better in semi-darkness and with candles alight in an otherwise dark room it becomes semi-dark. When it is dark or semi dark we become more alert which automatically raises the vibrations around us and helps Spirit to be recognised as being around. It is also necessary, if this exercise is going to work properly, for your armchair or comfortable seat to be placed at one end of the room with at least twelve inches of space behind it, and two of your candles to be placed strategically at the opposite end, one at each corner of the room, and the other two in the opposite corners of the room behind you. In other words your positions are like this:

LIT CANDLE   **LIT CANDLE**

CHAIR

LIT CANDLE   **LIT CANDLE**

(There should be approximately twelve inches of space behind the back of the chair and where the candles are placed.)

You need to be seated in the chair facing the two candles in front of you, and there being two candles behind you, which you have lit before taking your seat. The electric lights also need to be switched off.

1) Close your eyes gently, (in other words do not screw them up tightly.)

2) Turn your thoughts to someone you love who is in the Spirit World.

I would like to point out here that you are not calling that person up. We cannot call up the dead they have to want to visit and come of their own accord. This is simply to change your vibration to one of love which indicates to your Guardian Angel and other Guides that you only want people visiting you who come in love and light. Remember that for the Spirit World to help you they need direction from you, because you are the only person who has personal responsibility for your life, they do not. To do this, they rely very much on the vibrations that emanate from you to show them direction. Thinking of a person, whom you love in Spirit, emanates love, so they take this to mean that you are asking for people to visit in love, which is exactly what you are supposed to be doing. It is of course possible that the person who is in your thoughts will pay you a visit, but this is not because you called them up but purely because they were waiting for the light of love to emanate from you to give them permission to try and communicate with you properly. If this should happen at this stage then that is great, but please do not be disappointed if it does not, because I can assure you that your loved one whom you have in your vision is doing their best to help the procedure work whether it is directly or indirectly. Concentrate your thoughts on and about the person in Spirit whom you love, for as long as you feel comfortable, but remembering that this will need to be for a minimum of two minutes for it to stand any chance of giving the results that you are looking for.

3) Now open your eyes and immediately divert your right eye to the candle in front of you and on your right and the left eye to the

candle in front of you and on your left. (As you do this, try not to force yourself to see something because this will delay matters and not make them easier.)

4) At this stage just take a mental note of anything that has caught your eye. (This may be just a shadow or a flicker of light at this stage but do not worry about it.) And whilst thinking about this close your eyes again, at the same time as trying to keep the same thought in your vision. Try to keep this sight with you in your mind's eye for at least two minutes before quickly opening your eyes again and repeating the instructions in number four.

If you are following your instruction details correctly, you should be aware of more and more each time you follow them. Write down all the results in a note book to keep for reference until the next time. By doing this you will be able to see how much you are moving forward and how the results are changing.

It is a good idea not to spend too long doing this for your first attempt because this can encourage imagination to kick in thereby defeating the object of you making progress in the art of Spirit linking. I would suggest one hour at the most to begin with. This exercise helps to encourage the stimulation of your third eye which is essential for Clairvoyance (which is clear seeing of those in the Spirit World.) For this next exercise, although it is one where you can partake in the exercise whilst alone in the house, and as such do not need a partner, you do need to know some people, i.e.: family or friends whom you can talk to at a later date. Other than this you will only need some paper, scissors, a pen, a container to put your slip of paper into, and a note pad. Not forgetting of course that the room should be a darkened room with only enough light for you to be able to see.

Cut out several small pieces of paper approximately two inches by one inch. They should be all the same size as each other and there really needs to be at least five if you can manage it, although two would work, depending how many family members and friends you can involve. In other words you will need one piece of paper for each person with whom you can work and discuss the results with later.

On each piece of paper write the name of one of these people.

Shuffle your slips of paper whilst they are upside down so that you cannot see the names that are written on them.

Spread them out upside down in front of you, and choose one that you are drawn to.

Without looking, place the one you have chosen into your container and place it underneath your chair if possible or as near to the back of the chair behind your feet if it is the wrong type of chair and therefore does not have a gap underneath.

Before setting to work on this exercise, make sure that the remainder of the pieces of paper are out of the room or at least well away from where you are sitting; this is important to avoid confusion later on.

Now is the time to close your eyes and relax.

Try to clear your head as best as possible. I should remind you here that it is an impossibility to empty all thoughts out of your head, so please do not waste time trying. You can, however, just imagine that you can see the slip of paper that is beneath your chair. This is merely because as you concentrate on this your mind is less likely to wander.

As you relax you will start to see shapes and shadows at the back of your closed eye lids. This is good. Now is the time that thoughts or what appear to be thoughts will pop into your head. You need to try your best to remember what you were picturing and hearing.

As soon as you feel that the time is right, you should open your eyes and after taking a moment to acclimatise yourself back to the room, write down all the information that you have remembered.

Look at the name on the piece of paper under your chair. The name of the person written on this piece of paper is the person for whom the information should be for.

Next time you see that person tell them about it and see if they can understand what you have received. Even little things can turn out to be very important to that person. If you want to repeat the exercise a second time after you have written down all the information, this is okay. Remember to replace the piece of paper that you have already used into the pile before doing so, and brush your hand around the container to clear the vibrations from the previous name. If the same person should come out a second time it means that the Spirit World is desperately trying to contact that person to bring help to them.

If you are afraid that you will not remember things you can place a tape recorder nearby and say things out loud as you receive them. However it is still a good idea to write it down afterwards.

You are probably wondering how such a simple exercise could possibly help you with your Spiritual Development. It does help because it teaches you to link into Spirit's energy and vibration, towards someone who is not there with you. Remember that Mediums like myself conduct telephone readings for people far away whom we have never met. All we have is a name and sometimes the name is not the right one. This is when this part of your gift with linking will definitely come in handy. Yes, I know that you do not even have a name because you do not know what the piece of paper says, but this is necessary because you do know the people whose names are on your slips of paper so could be influenced by what you know instead of what you are being told. Also it is important to remember that when a Medium is on the rostrum they frequently do not know the person whom they are linking with and for. However, the way Spirit will work with you on these occasions is exactly the same. So practice it many times until you are confident with what you are doing. This exercise done, it is time to move forward to step two of this very important way of learning.

Once again shuffle your slips of paper whilst they are upside down so that you cannot see the names that are written on them.

Spread them out upside down in front of you once more, and this time choose three that you are drawn to.

Repeat the action without looking placing the ones that you have chosen into your container then place it underneath your chair if possible, but at the back of the chair if it is the wrong type of chair, and therefore does not have a gap underneath.

Once more make sure that the remainder of the pieces of paper are well away from where you are sitting, this is still important to avoid confusion later on, before setting to on this exercise.

Now it is back to the time to close your eyes and relax again.

Try to clear your head as best as possible. Just imagine that you can see the three slips of paper that are beneath your chair. I repeat, this is merely because as you concentrate on this, your mind is less likely to wander.

As you relax you will start to see shapes and shadows at the back of your closed eye lids. Now thoughts or what appear to be thoughts will pop into your head. You need to try your best to remember what you were picturing and hearing.

As soon as you feel that the time is right, you should open your eyes again and after taking a moment to acclimatise yourself back to the room, write down all the information that you have remembered.

Look at the names on the three pieces of paper under your chair. This once again should be for whom the information is for, but now you have to separate the information out so that you know what is for whom. Write each of the three names down on your pad and the information that you think corresponds with each person under their name. Remember processing the information is as important as the rest of the exercise.

When you next talk to these people you can check to see if your information is right. If not ask them if they understand any of the information that you thought were for the other two people on your list. Write down all the results so that you can cross check later.

Next it is important to work out where you went right or wrong in these two exercises. This exercise helps you to know when you are split linking and therefore helps you to learn not to do so.

I was at a Spiritualist Church on a day that Spirit had told me several weeks before that something good would happen to amaze and surprise me. As that day is reputed to be the luckiest day of the century I watched out all day for this amazing thing to take place but it did not appear to have done so, that is until I got a telephone call the following morning.

On the previous night I was giving a message to a lady in the Church whom had recently lost her husband to the Spirit World after he suffered a heart attack whilst driving occasioning him to have an accident of which the consequences meant surgery before he passed away to the Spirit side of life. The lady in question could take the whole of the message that Spirit communicated until I told her that there was a lady called Margaret who wished to speak to her. She answered that she did not know of a Margaret in the Spirit World or otherwise!!

To this the lady in Spirit said, that she lived next door to the lady's husband many years ago and again was next door recently and now. The message recipient did not understand and said she could not take it and as it was time for the service to finish, as reluctant as I was to do so I asked if she could try to check on the information and speak to me on a future visit? However, the following morning a friend of the lady, who had also been in Church the night before, telephoned me to let me know that when they went home after the service, they told the daughter of the recipient of the message that her father and some other Spirits had come through to talk to her mother that evening. Although the daughter did not really believe in the existence of those in the Spirit World she gasped with amazement when Margaret was mentioned.

She then relayed this story why.

The daughter and her husband had gone to visit her fathers grave the evening before whilst her mother was at Church. She said that as they stood next to her father's grave she was crying for the loss of her Dad which had only been approximately three weeks earlier. She looked up to see that there was a man who was standing by the next graveside and he was also crying. He apologised and told her that his wife had only recently died.

Once they got talking she learnt that his wife's name was Margaret and by coincidence or not!!

She had been in the next bed to her father and died within twenty four hours of him. After further discussion she found out that Margaret had been a neighbour of her father's many years earlier. Which is exactly what Margaret was relaying to her mother at the very same time as they were discussing it at the gravesides?

This was amazing just as Spirit had predicted don't you think?

Chapter Seven
A Message from Sun Flowers

7

A Message from Sun flowers

I have been lucky enough to be asked to perform Spiritual naming ceremonies on several different people, young and old alike. This, as the title suggests, is when a person takes part in a ceremony similar to one where a person would be christened into the Orthodox Church. The difference being that the person is given a Spirit name which connects close to their life pathway and gives them direction. As in a Christening, the person can be young or old when either they or their parents ask for the ceremony to be carried out.

At this point you may think that I am going off at a tangent but please bear with me because as you read on all will become clear to you as to why I am talking about a different subject for a moment. When I was a young child of about five or six years old, there was a strip of land about three feet wide between the footpath of my family home and the footpath of the house next door, which ran in parallel. My parents planted some large sunflowers along the middle of the strip of land for the full length of the foot path. Although I suspect that my Mum actually planted them because she was the gardener in our family and worked very hard to keep the gardens tidy and looking beautiful, just as she did our home. A few weeks after the flowers had been planted they bloomed into beautiful sun flowers reaching about three feet from the ground. They had huge beautiful heads and one day when my Dad had returned from work I went out into the garden with him, as I often did as a child. I remember looking in amazement at these flowers and asking my Dad why they were so big and bright? And secondly why they were called Sun flowers? My Father laughed as he usually did when I asked him what must have seemed like daft questions. Then he took my hand, looked down at me and explained that they were large and called Sun flowers because their beautiful bright faces absorbed the goodness from the sun so that it could be passed through the stem of the flowers and out through the roots to help the worms and creatures underground to stay strong and healthy. At that time I did not question whether my Dad's answers were right because I trusted him implicitly, so therefore my next question came out of my mouth quite quickly as usual. The question was: "I can't see any worms and creatures, where are they?"

Luckily my Father always tried his best to answer any questions that his children asked him. I remember him once telling me that we should never be ignorant to another soul because everyone is our equal and ignorance is a sign that you are not a very kind and sincere human being, because you are acting as though your own feelings are more important than the other person's and you should never do that because they are not. He told me that even the creatures should be treated well and if there was a reason to kill a tiny creature like an ant then you should do it quickly and painlessly. This day he explained to me that just because you cannot see something, it does not mean that it is not there. I must have looked puzzled because he went on to say that I would understand when I was older. (He could not have been more right if he tried could he?) He then went on to tell me that if ever I am sad I could look at the Sun flower, think of him, and all the good from these two things would make me happy.

A few days later I went up to my bedroom to find that a large patch of my bedroom wall surrounding the air vent was covered with literally hundreds of earwigs. I at once shouted for my Dad who luckily was home at the time. He told me to calm down because I was really excited and bothered by what I had seen and talking ten to the dozen. Once he had seen what all the excitement was about, he went downstairs and a few moments later came back with a large pot and a trowel. He moved my bed out of the way, which was positioned with the headboard under the air vent. Then he set to work, gently scraping the earwigs off the wall into the pot without hurting them. Once he was finished he took them, 'with me hot at his heels', to where builders were building a Church down the road from where we lived and released them into the field. He then returned home and taped up the air vent so that others could not crawl back in. This was the end of the subject, or so we thought!! That is until our next door neighbour came round to say that they had been having trouble with the earwigs too and the man said that they were coming from the Sun flowers so would he take them down? My Father of course knew that this would be the answer to the problem, as beautiful as the flowers were. So that afternoon after he had eaten his dinner, he set about the task of uprooting them. As I watched I started to cry. Dad immediately put down his spade to ask me why I was crying. I retorted in a tear stained voice that the hidden things would not stay strong and healthy without the Sun flowers and what would I do if I was sad, without them to look at, for help? He told me that the creatures would get help from other plants and that I could think of him and my old Dad (as he always put it) would bring help so that I know that the sun would shine in my life to bring new beginnings and when I saw a sunflower one day in the future it would be a message from my old Dad. This answer satisfied me, and from that day to this, whenever I see a Sunflower I think of my Dad and unseen things!! This is especially the case since he went to the Spirit World.

It was to be many years later whilst preparing for a Naming service in the USA that I came to realise the full meaning of those conversations about the Sun flowers that I had with my Dad. On the morning of the naming service I went out with the family to buy the flowers for the naming service that evening. The flowers are usually pink and white for Spiritual services because white is for purity from high Spirit and pink is for a Mother's love which is and always will be the strongest bond of love known to mankind. Therefore during services of Naming, Marriage, renewal of vows etc, pink is considered the colour to use, to bring that extra bond of love to the person or people involved.

After we had bought the flowers, the lady whose family was being named said that she would like to see if she could buy a sun flower. Of course my ears pricked up at this, and I asked: "Why do you want a sunflower?" She explained that the Mother of the Father of the baby, who was now in Spirit loved Sun flowers so she thought that it would be good to get one so that he would feel that she was close by. Unfortunately it was not to be because we could not find any sun flowers. So we decided to place his Mum's picture in a prominent position so that we could all see her and be reminded of her presence on that very important day.

Two days later I was at the Las Vegas Spiritualist Church and as soon as I walked through the door I saw a large framed picture of a Sunflower at the front of the Church, and some little Sunflowers growing in pots nearby. This obviously caught my immediate attention and when I got up to give messages from loved ones on the other side, I briefly told them about our search for a Sunflower two days earlier before the naming service, 'to represent the Baby's Dad's Mum who is in Spirit,' before I commenced with Spirit messages for those in the congregation. After the service had finished people from the congregation came over to talk to me as is usual after a service. One really nice lady came over and said to me that the day before whilst shopping she had been drawn to buy two candles in the shape of Sunflowers. She hurried on to say that she had never done anything like this before!! She then explained that she had forgotten to take them out of her bag and had the same bag with her that day. She continued. "After hearing what you said about the Sunflowers I decided to give one to you, but as I got it out of my bag I suddenly had the feeling that I should give you both." I thanked her sincerely, and briefly told her about the Sunflowers in my childhood. I said that if it was okay with her, I would keep one to take back to England as a message from my Dad but I would give one to the baby's Dad from his Mother. She was very pleased with this idea and I thanked her again. A few minutes later an elderly gentleman came up to me and said I have just been told by your Dad in Spirit to buy this CD for you. As he gave it to me, I noticed that it had the picture of a Sunflower covering the whole of one side. Turning it over bought a tear to my eye because of the title of the CD which was: '**Cosie The Other Side;** I took this to be the message from my Dad that he had promised all those years earlier, it told me that he is okay in the Spirit

World in a way that amazes even a Medium like me who has seen and does see my Father regularly, and as such I will treasure it forever. My greatest thanks go to both of those lovely Spiritual people. They have touched my heart and life forever.

All this happened in January 2007 and the lady who gave me the Sunflower shaped candles kept in touch. She was going to a workshop held by the lady called Cosie whose CD I had been given and asked if I would mind if she took a copy of my book to her and told her the story of the Sunflower and the unusual and special way in which my Dad and the Spirit World sent a message to a Medium whom they could just talk to if they so chose. I of course said yes this would be alright and she did just that. She said that Cosie hoped that one day we would get the opportunity to meet, and of course I agreed. She was travelling through Nevada again in June 2007 but it did not look as though there could be any possibility that I could be there, so that was the end of that, or so we thought!!! My sister was due to fly to Las Vegas but some problems arose and she said that her partner could not go at that time. Although I suggested Mike went, he felt that I should be the one to go, so I agreed to do this and Chris was to go with me. By coincidence, or not it was the very week when Cosie would be in Las Vegas where we were heading, so we did get to meet after all!!

The naming service itself is a very special and personal service to the family involved. This particular one was being held for four members of the family; the new born baby, and the baby's Mum, Dad, and Grandmother which obviously made the whole thing extra special for all involved including me. Although I should say that even if the naming service is only for one person, it is still really special. Like marriages these days, naming services can be held almost anywhere. It is usually left to the choice of the people who are involved. For instance, some people prefer it to be performed in Church whereas others prefer it to be performed in their home. Setting up the scene for the happy occasion it is good to make the venue look as spiritual as is possible. I have seen all sorts of set ups but I think the most beautiful one that I have attended is the one in the USA. On this particular occasion there were rows of seats for the people invited, to sit on and watch the ceremony which is obviously commonplace at these events. There was a large table set at the head of these chairs at which were placed four chairs. One for myself and one each for the Grandmother, Mother, and Father being Named, whilst of course the new born baby would be on a parent's lap.

On the table itself we placed four wide candles in a circular position, which would be lit as the service was due to commence. We then sprinkled a variety of crystal stones around the four candles, after which we placed a circle of unlit candles all around these in a circle. (Enough candles for one for every person present in the room) and finally we placed some quartz stones for love around the outside of the unlit candles. The scene was set and it looked not only beautiful but very spiritual indeed. As I have been asked by several of my readers, how I perform a naming service, I will now give a brief example. It is brief because the version I give here is somewhat condensed, whilst the main points are made so that you can gain an impression of what takes place. I have made up both the birth and Spirit names for this example and they do not connect to anyone. I will give an example of a naming service that I would do for a child and a naming service that I would do for an older child or adult. They are in fact similar but not the same,

Naming Service.

In starting a naming service, it is always important to extend a warm welcome to everyone present, especially the person or people being named and their loved ones. This should include mentioning that the service that is about to commence is on behalf of the person or people about to be named. At this point a lively song or hymn should be sung to help raise the vibrations and connect all those present together. An address is then given by me (or whoever is holding the service) as the Officiate, which is a talk showing the connection of those involved, to God, and the Spiritual growth of the person or people involved that will lead to God. The Officiate conducting the service should be a Medium. This is because later on in the service they will need to obtain a Spiritual name for the person or people being named from the Spirit World. It is also necessary during this address to welcome the person or people as a member of our Spirit Guided movement whilst praying for power that we may rightly serve their development in the ways of truth, love and Religion. We also ask for wisdom to order our actions that we need at no time be ashamed of the example we offer. But above all, we ask for the help and Guidance of the Spirit Teachers, that we may have the love, patience, and deep understanding which may serve these people in times of trial and strain.

Now as the Officiate I say, "let us pray," and say a prayer on behalf of the person or people being named.

I as the Officiate once again address the Parents, Family and Friends of the person or people being named, which basically tells these people their responsibilities to the named person or people, whilst asking them to let the named person's welfare and happiness be the challenge to their own highest nature. It asks them to remember their own weakness and need, and ask for the guidance of God and the High Spirit leaders, that they may have the strength by which they may train the soul being named to their care to the service of God and the well-being of man. The address finishes with:

"The love and grace of God are at your command, for in the very desire to secure and further the happiness of the person or people being named, you link self with these Divine Forces",

I as the Officiate now take the baby in my arms or place a hand on the right shoulder of the older person being named, asking, What name do you give this child/person? When the name is given, I say, whilst holding the pink and white flowers over the head of the person being named: These flowers......earth's purest gems.......are emblematic of that beauty and purity which God desires in the hearts of his children; In the name of God our Father and his Spirit Messengers I name this child/person the name of the person given at birth is quoted by the Spirit name of...... the Spirit name given from Spirit is now given.

May God bless and shield you, may His Spirit Messengers guide you, aid you in trouble, comfort you in sorrow, lead you into all truth, and may God's presence and blessing be with you throughout your life. The child should now be returned to its parent or the hand lifted off the older person's shoulder.

If there is more than one person being named, this last process should be repeated for each one. A second hymn or song can be sung here. Now it is time for the Officiate to say "let us pray", and say a prayer on behalf of the person or people being named and all those present. Then all shall say (or sing): the Lords prayer, (if appropriate to the family.) I now give the person/ people being named a message for their future from Spirit and tell them who in the Spirit World related to them was responsible for naming their Spirit Name. This is followed by a blessing:

Blessing.

May the blessing of God be on this person we call Birth name and on his/her parents, family and friends and, may all who enter their homes find in them the peace and love which will pass all understanding.

I would now like to say that as Birth name of person who has been named whose Spirit name is: Spirit name come forward amongst their family and friends, light one of the candles in the circle whilst making a personal blessing for the named person/people. After which, please step back from the table holding your lit candle until everyone present has a lighted candle. Once this is done I ask everyone to close their eyes whilst I say a blessing from us all to the named person/people. After which I say they can all blow out the candle and keep it as a keepsake of this special day if they wish to do so and now those who wish to do so can give a single flower to the named person/people and are permitted to take photographs.

Thank you, God Bless you all.

Chapter Eight
More So Called Coincidences

8

More So Called Coincidences?

It was late afternoon one Sunday when whilst chewing a piece of what appeared to be soft chicken, the whole front of a back tooth crumbled away. This puzzled me because I could not understand what had made it crumble. I can actually imagine you now thinking: 'What has this got to do with Spirit?' Well please read on and all will be revealed.

I arrived at Chris' about an hour later and by then my toothache was throbbing nicely. I telephoned the dentist thinking that they would give me a number for an emergency dentist as had always been the case in the past. However the rules have changed and you now phone a number and wait in a huge queue whilst music plays intermittently alternated by an advertisement about their web site, which as you can imagine is very annoying when you are suffering a lot of pain and telephoning to try and get help. Finally a lady came on the line, asked a lot of questions and gave me a new number to ring a dental nurse for advice. I am a very placid person but by this time I was in even more pain and getting a little agitated to say the least. I did not need advice; I needed treatment because it does not take a dentist to tell you that if the front of your tooth has fallen off and the nerve is exposed, that you will have pain until a dentist has repaired it. Anyway I telephoned the dental nurse's number as instructed and because the chemists were all closed, it being a Sunday evening which meant I could not buy a temporary filling which was their first advice, I was then told to take some pain killers to ease the pain alternated with anti-inflammatory tablets. She also gave me four telephone numbers of dentists near to my home whom would perform emergency treatment if I called them the following morning. When I came off the telephone I was not impressed because I had already taken pain killers an hour earlier and they were not helping. So there I was abandoned to suffer all night by what is supposed to be a caring nation. I told Spirit what I thought and they answered there is a reason why you need to go for treatment tomorrow. I remarked to Chris which dentist I was drawn to on my newly acquired list, but said that I guess I should try the others first because that one was the furthest away from my home. When nine-o-clock the next morning came around and I knew that the dentist would be open I started to ring the numbers on my list. Firstly I was told three pm the next day, then I was told by the next two four and four thirty pm respectively on Thursday. Remember that it was now Monday and I had been awake all night in agony!! Next I telephoned the one that I had shown preference for the night before. They agreed to see me at three pm that afternoon so I agreed.

Upon arrival at the dentist I was greeted by a very nice polite lady in a Nurse's uniform who asked me to fill in a form, which I duly did and returned it to the reception office. As I walked into the reception area, I was met with the sight of some business cards with the name of the accompanying part of the practice facing out on the desk. The card read: WOW FACTOR. I gasped with surprise and the Nurse asked me if I was all right? I quickly explained the circumstances of how I came to be there that day and added that I am a Medium by profession and am constantly billed as the Medium with the WOW FACTOR. I added this has to be an omen. She replied, "well I do not know about that but you are just what I need".

I had my tooth dealt with and was pleased with the treatment and the whole dental practice. Then I went back to the Nurse and was able to help by easing her mind a little about a recent loss under very sad circumstances. Now I knew why I had to wait for the next day to see a dentist and indeed why I had been drawn to the dentist with the WOW FACTOR. Very fitting don't you think, that a Medium with the WOW FACTOR should have her teeth looked after by a dentist with the WOW FACTOR!!!? What do you think? Coincidence or God and Spirit having a quiet word with me to bring help to a very kind and special individual in trouble? I know what I think.

Whilst travelling on a recent trip to America, Chris and I booked in only to find that because we had booked the tickets on line, they had seated us, not only at opposite sides of the plane but I was also a lot further back than Chris. We asked as we were boarding if anything could be done about this because after all it was an eleven hour flight and we would obviously prefer to keep each other company. I was told to look for a young lady of a certain name which I will not divulge because of anonymity and ask her if she could help.

We boarded the plane and Chris took her seat whilst I went round to the back of the other side of the plane and stood waiting for this stewardess to happen along. A steward asked why I was standing and unfortunately was not very helpful at all and asked me to take my seat. Luckily for me the young lady whom I had been asked to look out for walked past at precisely that moment, so I called out to her. After explaining my predicament she told me to wait and she would ask around to see if anyone would be willing to change seats so that Chris and I could sit together for the long flight. She did also explain that she could not make anyone move and the flight was full. She asked around and periodically came back to tell me that she had had no luck so far but that she would keep trying. One time when she returned she said to me, people can be difficult you know, they are not all the same. I told her that I realised this because, I too worked with the public.

She asked what I do and I told her that I was an Author and a Medium which piqued her interest and she immediately replied whilst waving her hands in the air: "Can you see anything with me?" My response was at first to laugh because if I was paid a pound for every time someone had said that to me I would be worth a fortune. Quite often when this happens, I tend to answer: "Yes I could do but I am not working now." But in this instance I decided that she was going out of her way to try to find someone to exchange seats for me so therefore the very least I could do was to give her a message from her Father who had died three weeks earlier and knew about a private matter that she was puzzling about and wanted to offer her his guidance. I told her what I was being told and she was so pleased that she started to cry. She went off to dry her eyes then she came back and told me that she had found a young gentleman who would change seats with Chris so that we would at least be on the same side of the plane as me.

Chris came over and told me to sit in the gentleman's aisle seat because of my bad leg and she would sit in my middle seat. We had just taken our new seats when Chris remembered that the lady who had been sitting by her originally had said that if I had an aisle seat she would swap. The stewardess went over to ask her if she would now move and she said yes, then she asked the young man who was a true gentleman if he would swap again so that we could sit together and he did. These people are the sort of people who renew your faith in human nature don't you think? Happily we were able to sit together for the rest of the journey but that was not the end of this amazing true story that makes you pleased to be alive.

Just before the meal came round Chris asked the other Stewardess if it was possible to buy a small bottle of Champagne to have with her meal instead of the free bottle of wine that is usual on these flights. She said that unfortunately they did not do that any more and went about her business. A few minutes later when Chris went to use the toilet she saw the two Stewardesses, the one who had helped with the seating arrangements and the one whom Chris had asked about the Champagne. They handed her two small bottles of Champagne and said that they had managed to get it from the other part of the plane and that there was one bottle for Chris and one for me to have with our lunch. Chris explained that I do not drink alcohol but said that she would have one bottle for herself and pay for it. They insisted that she took both without payment and said that she could either drink them both with her lunch or take them off with her. She replied that she did not think that she was allowed to carry liquid off because of the restrictions at that time but she was reassured that she could take it off because she had been given it by them whilst on the plane. A few hours later, I felt someone rubbing my shoulder and looked up to see the Stewardess who had helped us smiling at me as she handed a full bottle of Moet Champagne over to Chris and said: "Jean told me earlier that your daughter is expecting her first baby soon so this is to wet the baby's head". She then smiled at me again and said "thank you very much Jean, as soon as I get back to England I will buy a copy of your book". This sort of thing always touches my heart because on many occasions people tend to just take Spirit and me for granted and she had clearly not done this. Chris and I would like to meet her again to tell her the rest of the story about the Champagne's journey to its final destination to wet the baby's head because the story is a funny one.

On our way through to Las Vegas where Chris' daughter lives we went to San Francisco for three days. During this brief stay Chris had time to drink the remaining small bottle of Champagne but obviously could not drink the full bottle in that time all by herself. We discussed whether or not we thought that it would be okay to take it on the plane to Las Vegas and to her daughter and decided that we would put it in her suitcase and take a chance that it would be okay in the hold. This was fine until we were walking along the corridor from the aeroplane in Vegas Airport and we suddenly heard Chris' name being called out over the tannoy to go to the information desk immediately. I looked at Chris and she had gone white. I told her not to worry because I would come with her and help her to explain where the Champagne had come from and if necessary they could throw it away. However, the more we heard her name being called the more nervous we both became about the whole thing. We arrived at the desk and the lady told Chris that there was someone here to speak to her. We were both very nervous at this point but there was no need to be because it turned out that Chris' daughter was not at work after all and had come to meet us. So therefore the champagne was used for exactly what it was intended for, to wet the baby's head by way of thanks from the Stewardess and her Dad in Spirit. Can you imagine at some point in the future, if I tried to bring that story through to a Medium for someone? It was confusing enough whilst it was happening.

As I have said many times before, it is never safe or a good idea to use the Ouija board without a qualified Medium being present, but as both Mike and I are qualified Mediums we occasionally do use it with friends.

One Friday evening we decided to do just that. Our friend Chris' Dad came through and told us that he would be coming with us on our day out. As our plan was to use the May day bank holiday Monday to visit Cardiff Castle, Mike replied "Oh you are coming to Cardiff Castle with us are you? Because that is where we plan to go this coming Monday." He immediately answered "ARE YOU?" in an enquiring type of voice, then promptly said goodbye before we could question him any further. We all laughed about this and the subject was put out of our minds. That is until the following Monday!!!

On the Sunday evening before our trip Chris suggested that we should look up Cardiff Castle on the internet and get the post code to feed into my 'Tom Tom Sat Nav' for the next day's journey, to make sure that we knew where we were going. I did just that and Chris wrote the post code down. I fed the information into my 'Tom Tom' from the piece of paper that Chris had written the previous night, on the morning of our journey we happily set off towards Cardiff Castle, or so we thought!!!

It is not unusual for the 'Tom Tom' to take us on an alternative route to our usual direction to begin with, so we took no notice when it did just that. However, we travelled and travelled and travelled!!! Although we started to wonder which way we were being directed we decided that we were too far into our journey at that point to turn round and head in a different direction, so we persevered and persevered until after over five hours of travelling we noticed a sign which indicated that we were thirty eight miles from London. ' I should point out here that it only takes two and a half hours to reach central London from my home and it had taken us over five hours to reach thirty eight miles away from the outskirts of London.

At this point it was suggested that we should pull off the motorway and stop to check where the 'Tom Tom' was taking us because it definitely was not heading for Cardiff or anywhere near it come to that. Once stopped, I removed the 'Sat Nav' from the car window and pushed the right buttons to indicate our final destination. We were horrified to see Rochester staring back at us, which is indeed the other side of London. I immediately delved into my handbag, which like most women's handbags is like a bottomless pit. After several minutes search I pulled out the piece of paper that Chris had written the post code to Cardiff Castle on. Checking it with the post code that I had plugged into the 'Tom Tom' I realised that I had put the wrong code in even though I had got Chris to check it for me at the time I put it in.

The reason for this mistake was because Chris was brought up in Holland she had been taught to write her Fs with a cross bar across the top like our Ts and a tiny stroke for the bottom stroke of the F. I glanced at this and saw a T not an F which it should have been. Chris and I laughed when we realised what had happened but Mike, who is not the most patient of people, was not at all impressed. I said that it was not Chris' fault, it was mine because she cannot help the way she writes, but I should have been more careful to read it properly. Chris said that it was equally not my fault because I read it in the way that I had been taught. Mike however, did not agree and said that it was both of our faults and indicated that we should go home now because we had been out over five hours and had had our day out. We did not agree with this idea because we felt that we had not been anywhere. So Chris suggested that we go into London and catch a show. After seven hours of travelling we arrived in central London where it took us another hour to find a parking place and we missed the matinee showing.

Mike was not impressed but he was a lot happier when after deciding to stay and watch the night time showing of 'Les Misérables' he found it to be a brilliant show as did we. It is also very interesting don't you think that the show we saw has Spiritual connotations and Chris' Dad when told that we were going to Cardiff Castle had replied 'Are you?' in an enquiring tone of voice as if to question where we were going, and he is the Dutch member of Chris' heritage and therefore indirectly responsible for the way she writes her Fs like Ts.

He obviously planned where we should really go that day and put his plans into action. It is also interesting that I had always wanted to see that Show and Chris had seen the Show before and had always said that she would like to see it again, because the first time she saw it she had not realised its Spiritual connotations; probably because she was not so spiritually aware at the time she first saw it. That trip will always go down in our memories as the day Chris' Dad planned our mystery tour day out for us and in the end a good time was had by all.

I know that this will then bring the question into your mind:

"What happened to personal responsibility and them not taking control of our lives?"

Well as I said I had always wanted to see that show and had made this clear as a future intention in the past, which gives them my permission. It had also originally been my choice where we went that day and I should also add that my bad leg was playing up and swollen that day so therefore I was better placed at the theatre than walking about castles on that particular occasion, don't you think?

Chapter Nine
Dreams

9

Dreams

"I have a dream," is a title of a song that I am very fond of, yet it is something that every living being has in common with each other. From a very early age we daydream about something that we would like. For instance, I should imagine that as a young baby we very quickly learn that the hunger pangs that we feel in our tummy means that we require to be fed. This in turn makes us think about our bottle and we start to cry to be fed. This is a very basic example of how people use their senses from a very early age. We are then taught how to play and it does not take long before we are trying to get hold of a toy we can see that is out of reach. You can see from the look of excitement on a baby's face at this point that they are almost yearning to get hold of that toy. Have you ever noticed that if you turn your back for a moment on a baby in this position, they have suddenly managed to get hold of the very toy that they could not reach? I believe that the reason for this is because at this early age our ability to day-dream interacts with our ability to sleep dream, therefore enabling us to link with the Spirit World from that very early and fragile age.

I should at this point reiterate that the Spirit World, live in the same space as we do but on a much faster vibration. This faster vibration is reachable by LOVE, which babies have naturally in copious amounts. They merely send out a loving desire to get hold of what they want, whilst getting excited in anticipation of reaching the toy that they can see and so desperately require to get hold of, and hey presto they are linking to Spirit.

When a baby is so small and vulnerable, their Guardian Angel stays extremely close to help when requested, which means that their desire to reach a toy has been noted and this is where Spirit are able to dematerialise (or make disappear) that toy which like everything else is made up of molecules, and re-materialise (make it reappear) it close to the baby so that he or she can now reach it. You may be now thinking 'well how does this help the baby when the toy had been deliberately placed out of reach to encourage the child to crawl and get it?' The answer to this is that it makes the baby realise that by extending their senses they can reach out for what they want. This in turn encourages them to stretch out and learn new ways of moving.

As we get older, the desire to have a toy that another child has got, encourages us to develop the daydream part of our character to develop too; the wish and desire that a latest toy etc could maybe be ours. At this stage a lot depends upon the character and development of skills as to whether our daydreaming ability to link to Spirit grows. This is because the way to connect with Spirit is through love. A spiteful child who just takes what he or she wants from another child in a bullying way loses their ability to daydream their way forward to some extent. This is the start of where good always wins over evil, because daydreaming develops our skill to reach out for what we want in life and not expect it to just come to us, thereby, developing our sixth sense at the same time. Although babies definitely dream, it would be hard for anyone to establish how vivid these dreams are, but babies definitely smile a lot, both in sleep and waking hours in a direction where it looks to the average person as though there is nothing or no one to smile at. We are more able to research these things the older a person becomes.

People who daydream regularly are stretching their senses, including their sixth sense. It quite often occurs that thoughts come into a person's head providing a way to move forward with a particular aspect of their life whilst daydreaming. This is because when we daydream we think lovingly about something that we desire, which in turn changes our vibration onto the right vibration for the Spirit World to communicate with us, thereby advising us of a way forward. Remember the key to where Spirit reside is the 'Light Of Vibration Eternity,' which is: LOVE? Unfortunately, people frequently do not realise that this is what they are doing, therefore daydreaming remains just that, daydreaming. However, the same does not usually apply to dreaming whilst we are asleep. Everyone dreams whether they are aware of it or not. Whilst asleep we are on the same vibration that a Medium is on when they are linking to the Spirit World. This enables our Guardian Angel, Guides, Helpers and Spirit visitors to communicate with us during this time. May I just point out that because Spirit reside on the vibration of love, this is the vibration that is linked into whilst we are asleep, therefore evil Spirits cannot reach us at these times.

I can just imagine that your thoughts have gone directly to nightmares as you are reading this. These have nothing to do with evil Spirits. It is, usually the fact that the person is trying to deal with problems within their life and they have fallen asleep thinking about them, therefore their brain is trying to make sense of this information. Unfortunately the human brain dreams back to front and upside down, which jumbles up any information that we receive at these times. The bigger the problems the more anxious the dreamer becomes and this changes the jumble into a nightmare.

Nightmares are in fact rarely Spirit orientated, but when they are, the principle of reversal applies. In other words the things that happen in the nightmare are the opposite of what you are being made aware of in reality. Where dreams are concerned, the more vivid they are in your memory when you awake, the more likely it is that Spirit were communicating with you, However, the same rule applies about being jumbled, therefore they usually need to be analysed.

A part of the Chinese culture has developed a way to reach within for strength by summoning their "chi" This ability basically allows a normally weak person to gain physical strength within their body. The same principle applies when we are attempting to change our vibration to link with the Spirit World. This is achieved by relaxing down inside which automatically raises your vibration. The idea, just like the principle of summoning your chi, is to make your body go so relaxed that it is almost floppy, whilst at the same time sending love out into the ethers and receiving it back again. When we are asleep we go through this process naturally.

Whilst practising the exercises in this book we are going to be encouraging Spirit to talk to us through our dreams because this is a way that it is easy for them to communicate with us. This as I have said before is because whilst asleep we are on the same vibration that Mediums are on when they link to Spirit. This is the vibration where "the so-called-dead", live; making each living person easily accessible for communication to and from the Spirit World as long as they have the desire to hear them and learn. Here are a few examples of dreams and their analysis to help you to understand more as you develop this faculty which is available to every living being.

DREAM 1:

Dream:
I dreamed that I was a passenger in the front seat of my friend's car when we turned down a very narrow one way street. There was approximately six inches to spare at each side of the car. We were chatting away happily when I noticed that there was a large car coming down this narrow one way street in the opposite direction. Chris started to brake and was sounding her car horn to alert the other driver that he was going to hit us.

Analysis:
This dream was telling me that at that moment in my life events that were occurring were making me feel hemmed in and stifled.

Dream:
He, however, took no notice and kept coming. We were almost stopped when this car collided into us head on, but as it did so the car mounted up on the bonnet of the car that we were in just as though it was going to drive over the top of our car. We could not escape because there

was not enough room for the doors to open to let us out. As the car crashed through the front window screen, it appeared to be travelling in slow motion until it came to a halt on top of my chest and I was aware that I could hardly breathe and the car was collapsing more and more and putting more pressure on my chest wall all the time. I was desperately trying to push the car away but it was too heavy and would not budge.

Analysis:
The car coming straight at us and on top of me indicates that the way to tackle the problem is head on. But the fact that it did not go right over the top indicates that the problems will appear to be insurmountable but can be resolved by me.

Dream:
I called out to Chris "Are you ok?" The answer came back "Don't worry they will get us out soon". I replied "Chris help me I am being stifled here, I cannot breathe. Please help me." At that point I woke up.

Analysis:
The fact that Chris was there giving reassurance is saying that I should not worry because although my worries are making me feel stifled I am not alone because good friends are around to help and support me in my time of need so therefore I would be alright.

DREAM 2:

Dream:
I dreamed that I had flies in my hair after going under a bush.

Analysis:
The flies in the hair on my head indicated that lots of problems were buzzing around me at that time.

Dream:
Chris and I were going to work together and we walked into a factory.

The boss immediately put Chris to work on an assembly line where the cake type cups were coming down a slope and she had to fill them as they went past. She was doing a really good job and enjoying herself so I asked if I could have a go? The boss told me that I would need to go round to the back of the machine on my right where I would find Martin working.

Analysis:
Chris and I going into the factory to work together meant that changes were due to take place in both of our lives. (It does not imply that I should stop being a Medium and become a factory worker.) Chris working happily and so well on this new task with the added fact that the assembly line was coming down hill so was therefore moving faster tells us that she will cope very well and easily with any changes in her life and be really happy with the changes. Myself, asking if I could join in says that I will also take well to the changes. I have a brother Martin so this tells me I will be in familiar surroundings.

Dream:

Chris said I could not do that so he pointed out of the window to her left where there was a row of blue mini cars and he said, "Otherwise you can go and wash some cars." Chris replied, "can I go and wash some cars?"

Analysis:
Being told to go and work around the corner and Chris disagreeing and suggesting that she and I wash some cars meant that she would always look out for me. The row of mini cars was because the mini is a car that is a combination of the past, the present and the future as was our new life. They were blue because blue is for communication, saying that this would be a large part of our new lives and washing the neat row of blue cars meant that our communication would always be above board, orderly and correct, straight from Spirit. Remember Spirit work well close to water.

DREAM 3:

Dream:
On Tuesday 8th October 2005 I dreamed that my friend Chris and I were going to visit a lady whom I knew through the Spiritualist Church. We arrived at what I thought was the flat where she lived and opened the door which led to the stairwell up to her flat. However after climbing the flight of stairs we found out that it was the wrong flat, so returned down the stairs and headed down the road to the end of the next block of flats because I remembered that she lived in a flat at the end of the block. As we walked down the road I could see another lady whom I knew from a Church much further away, talking to a crowd of people but she did not see or hear me.

Analysis:
This dream is clearly a precognitive dream intended to direct me in the right direction in life. First of all in the dream Chris and I were looking for a particular flat and a particular lady. The dream was relaying to me that you should never narrow your chances in life down to just travelling in one direction, unless you know it to be the right one. Secondly, the lady whom I was searching for never materialised but other similar people were there instead. This was telling me that sometimes you cannot take the people whom you meet on your pathway at face value so you should watch for this. This theme carried on throughout the dream which was trying to bring the point home to me.

Dream:
Arriving at the next block we noticed that you had to go in through a gangway at the side of the petrol garage and up some stairs. I commented that although we would look I did not think that this was the one because I did not remember the layout. After clambering up the steep stairwell we came to a dirty looking white door with a bell in the centre and although I knew, beyond a shadow of a doubt, that this flat did not belong to the lady whom we were trying to visit, I pressed the doorbell so that we could enquire about the lady we were looking for. As soon as my finger hit the button the door flew open and there lying

on the doormat behind the door was a large hairy dog. He jumped up immediately and out of the door which made us jump but there was no need to worry, because he did not bother us at all, in fact there was not even a bark.

Analysis:
Thirdly, the dream was saying that you should take the pathway of least resistance which would make your journey through life so much easier and also that you should go with your first decision and not change your mind, then everything will go well.

Dream:
A young lady approximately in her twenties appeared at the door and although I did not know her personally, she was the spitting image but a younger version of a lady whom I know well that belongs to the same Church as the lady I was really looking for. This startled me a bit but before I had the chance to say anything she said "Hello come in" and returned into the room behind a screen type wall. As I stepped into the hallway I heard the sound of someone eating and as I walked around the screen I saw that the lady was now lying on a sofa under a blanket with a man. They were lying top and tail style and I asked if they were eating their lunch to which the man replied "Yes" because his partner's sister was visiting in an hour. (Her sister was the lady whom looked like the one that I knew, yet in reality I only know the lady at the Church and not the younger sister who I was speaking to). I apologised and Chris and I headed back towards the stairwell from which we had come.

Analysis:
The fact that Chris was with me when she works alongside me spiritually in life says that she will be there for the long haul no matter what obstacles come in our way. These people carrying on with their food as they spoke to me is saying that you should not let interruptions get in the way of important tasks. Meeting the sister who is like the lady I was looking for indicates that there is always more to a person than you at first see and you should always look deeper. This includes

when you are linking to someone in the Spirit World.

Dream:
However as we arrived at the top of the stairs there were now two flights instead of one. We chose the stairs on the right and Chris went down first. At this point I was aware that I now had crutches and knew that the stairs were too steep for me to attempt to go down using them so I slid the crutches down the stairs and they disappeared at top speed.

Analysis:
Me sliding the crutches down the stairs and managing without them or help from Chris to get down the stairs tells me that I will regain my full health after all the surgery that I have undergone in the past two years. Therefore overall this dream is a lucky one that says if I choose with care and not get directed into other directions in my life at the suggestion of other people then I will do extremely well.

Dream:
Once outside again and back in the car I became aware that I was now driving, yet at that time in reality, I could not drive after surgery on my knee.

Analysis:
I would be well enough to drive again in the future.

Dream:
Just up the road we came to a fork in the road and it was not too clear which one would keep us on the road which we were travelling. I contemplated taking the right fork but at the last minute changed my mind and took the left one instead. This road was very narrow and winding in comparison to the one which we were previously travelling upon, so I knew it was the wrong one almost immediately but there was nowhere to turn around for some distance. After a while I saw a car parked off to my right and told Chris that I must stop for a call of nature so we parked the car and walked over to the car park

in search of a toilet. We clambered down a slippery bank and realised that it was time to turn back and take the right fork because this way was extremely difficult whether we were in the car or walking. At that point I woke up.

Analysis:
The first thing that comes into your head is the right thing to do. The dream was reiterating that we were following the right pathway in life and should keep going, instead of choosing the difficult route. Therefore even if you are uncertain you should keep going with your first instinct. But if you do not do this and you realise that you have made a mistake then turn back and rejoin your right pathway as quickly as you can and learn by your mistakes that you now know caused you problems. I should say to you that I did make a full recovery from all my surgery.

Hopefully you are starting to get used to using your dream cards so now I think that it is the ideal time to start mixing the dream card reading and the dream analysis together as one. Just simply relax and follow these instructions and you will be surprised at how much of a boost your confidence will get once you realise that you are moving forward with your development. As you are ready to settle down to sleep at night, take the box of cards into your hands, close your eyes and whilst gently rubbing the cards ask: Please show me my direction? (You do not need to speak out loud for your Guardian Angel, Guides, and helpers to hear you, because they are permanently tuned in to your questions and needs to some degree or another. Just think the question very clearly), Once you have asked the above question, open your eyes for a few seconds, and place the cards back down where you keep them close to your bed. Lie down in the position that you use to drift off to sleep, close your eyes once more and think the question again: Please Show me my direction? Now keeping your eyes lightly closed, look into the darkness that comes from closing your eyes to the world and try to remember what you see. It does not matter if you fall asleep before you go very far as long as you have followed these instructions which will only take you a minute or so to complete. As soon as you wake up in the morning, open the cards, take them out of their box and shuffle them whilst once again thinking the question: **Please Show me my direction?**

Place the pack of cards down somewhere like on the bed or bedside table and pick up as few or as many of the cards off the top of the pack as you feel drawn to. Look at the card that is now on the top of the pile of cards that are in your hand then write down the number starting with the number one on the first night, two on the second night etc. after first writing the date. (The date will be important later on.) Then write the word or words that are the heading of that card, on a fresh page in your pad. Place all the cards back in the pack. Leave a space then write down anything that you saw the night before whilst your eyes were shut before you went to sleep. If you only saw a white shadow or a colour, then write it down because it will be significant. There is no such thing as 'only' when we are dealing with anything that we see, hear or sense, when practising to develop our Spiritual gifts.

I would like you to remember, so that you do not get too frustrated, that you should never compare your development to anyone else' ability. This is because as I have said before in my other books, we are all psychic to varying degrees but we cannot all be great Mediums. I believe that Mediums are born. This, however, does not mean that you cannot develop to a very satisfying level of awareness in a way that you will believe without a doubt in life after death and to a degree that the Spirit World will be able to help you in a positive way with your life.

Now draw a line under what you have written, ready to carry on with day two the following bedtime. I am asking you to repeat this procedure for three consecutive nights. After these three nights are done, you will need to wait until you have a little time to spare because you may need at least half-an-hour, to an hour, for the next stage of the exercise. If that is that same morning then that is fine but if it is five or six days later then that is also fine. Make yourself comfortable and have your tools close at hand. It is also a good idea to have a small table or clear surface available for this part of the exercise. Now find all three cards from the pack and place in a pile in the order they were picked. (If a card was duplicated twice or more then you will obviously have less than three cards in your pile. However, you will know which places the duplicated cards belong to by looking at the number one to three of each night on your pad. Turning to a fresh page on your pad or using another pad if it is easier. Write down the sentence written on the bottom of card one. For instance if your first chosen card was card two it would be:

Card 2 =ABUNDANCE IS YOURS.

Now write what you saw when your eyes were shut that night. Do this for all three cards in succession so that it reads a bit like an essay on your pad. CONGRATULATIONS! you have made your first short prediction for your life without any outside help apart from my book and dream cards. Now sit back and watch as it comes true because this will give you confidence to help you move forward with your ability to use your intuitive side to gain information from the so-called-dead!!!

Chapter Ten
Dream Talk from My Guides

10
Dream Talk from My Guides

Spirit sometimes get frustrated with people like myself who are quite capable of listening to their communication but tend to use it for the benefit of other people, paying less attention when it is meant as guidance for me. During the course of a spell of extreme bad health, spirit decided to go back to basics and express a dream to me to say what they thought I needed to be told.

DREAM 1
I dreamed that I had been visiting a close friend whose son had recently passed to Spirit.

Analysis.
Therefore I was being shown that he was helping me from Spirit to thank me for trying to help his family.

Dream:
My husband Mike and Daughter Toni were with me in the dream, and we stopped to pay a visit to a public toilet in a nearby Town Centre. Both the male and female toilets were in the same building, which we had to climb a flight of stairs to reach. As we reached the top of the stairs, I noticed that the walls were covered in large reddish coloured tiles. Turning to the right, there was a doorway in front of us with the word 'Gentlemen' written above it, and the tiles on the walls through that doorway were small and white like you would find in most public conveniences. To the left and down a small passageway, there was a really wide door with the word 'Ladies' written above it. However the tiles in the ladies were large

and red, just as they were at the top of the stairs. Mike went into the gents, and Toni opened the wide door, which, was the ladies. She turned to me and exclaimed:

"Oh, it really stinks in here and there is water everywhere!"

At that I replied:

"You go in and I will wait here for you."

Analysis.
Remember the wall tiles were reddish in colour, which is because he was aware that I needed strength at that time. The gents had white tiles because Mike himself was safe. I was at the public convenience, yet not where the toilets were? In other words, Spirit was indicating that I was communicating with Spirit but not asking the necessary questions to get the help that I needed?

Dream
With this remark, I placed my bags down on the floor, leaning against the wall near the entrance to the Gents. I had two bags, one of which was a carrier bag and the other was my handbag. Strangely though, the handbag was one that I had used to its full capacity and discarded twelve months previous to the dream. It was originally a birthday present from two close and much loved friends, Sue and John. However, it had worn out, and therefore was no longer used. At this point in the dream, I heard footsteps coming up the stairs behind me. I turned to see a slim, wiry looking gentleman of a scruffy appearance enter the space at the top of the stairwell. I could not help but notice how thin and unkempt his hair was? He strode past me towards the large door that was the Ladies, so I said:

"Excuse me, but that is the Ladies, the Gents are over there."

I was pointing towards the door to the gentlemen's toilets as I did so. He glanced at me momentarily, then looked down to the floor where my bags were. Then suddenly without warning, he strode forward to attack me.

Analysis

There was water all over the floor in the ladies which was saying that they had been trying really hard to make me see the dangers and things to avoid in my life but I was standing back from that information. I let the water and the fact that it smelt badly put me off going into the toilet block itself, which was the right thing to do because we would have both been in a more vulnerable position if he had come in to the block where we were both out of sight, but I should have also listened to the message that Spirit were trying to give to me by showing the flood of water. I spoke to the man who had turned towards the ladies, 'thinking that I was being of help' yet in reality I had drawn his attention to me and my bag and put myself in danger. This tells me that at times you cannot help the other person and just get drawn into their troubles if you try, so therefore it is wise to stand back and pay attention to what you need yourself instead of always worrying about other people's troubles. Toni and I should in fact not have entered the toilet block but gone back downstairs to street level where we would have been safer. The fact that I was using a bag that was now in reality worn out, and had originally been given to me by close friends was saying that I am always loved and protected by close friends.

The suddenness of this within the dream caused me to awaken from my sleep with a start. As I rubbed my eyes and recovered from what turned out to be a bad dream, I became aware that Mike was making some strange noises in his sleep lying next to me. At that moment he moved suddenly and quite quickly, which unfortunately made him fall out of bed. Once he had recovered from the shock he told me the content of his dream.

DREAM 2, MIKE'S DREAM

He dreamed that he and I were looking around this really big house. There was stuff strewn everywhere, all over the place, in every room. He went into the bathroom to find that the toilet was missing? On going downstairs to use that toilet, he found that that one too was conspicuous by its absence. Turning to me he exclaimed:

"Someone has pinched all the loos in this house."
It was at this point that he had fallen out of bed, bringing an abrupt end to his dream.

First of all before I start to analyse this dream for you, can I remind you that Mike and I were dreaming these dreams containing toilets, simultaneously. If you have already read my two previous books, or know me personally, then you will already be aware that whenever I go to use the toilet, Spirit take the opportunity to talk to me because they know that I will allow this, and Spirit communicate better whilst using the energy produced by water?

<u>Analysis of Mike's Dream.</u>
This dream was in fact a very easy one to interpret. It was a big house which is telling him that his opportunities are vast. Yet things were strewn all over the house which indicates that everything is too messed up in his life for him to be able to see what he should do. The toilet being missing was telling him that things were not conveniently placed in his life for him to be able to make use of what should in fact be easy for him. Going downstairs to find this toilet was also missing was saying that even when things are made easy for him, (hence going downstairs not up) he still was not using all the help that was available to him. We were dreaming about toilets at the same time because we were at that time pulling in opposite directions instead of the same one. Mike went in the opposite direction in my dream because he entered the toilet block on the right. The toilets in my dream were usable if you were desperate but not very nice. Therefore jointly this dream was saying that he should learn to pull in the same direction then he can take advantage of what is available to him instead of heading for a fall. (He did in fact fall out of bed didn't he!!!?)

A premonition dream that I had recently, appeared to be confusing to the ordinary everyday eye on the subject but it was obviously a premonition for me, and here it is:

DREAM 3

I was attending a wedding and having a good time when I went out through this large hallway to go to the toilets.

Analysis.

The fact that I was at a wedding, so was obviously seated, with people I knew, but had ventured out into the large hallway alone to find the toilets, is indicating that although people have been and are around to help, I need to push forward on my own, whilst knowing friends were close in a situation around me at that moment.

Dream

A woman stopped me to say hello, and asked if I was related to one of the couple getting married? I replied that I was a friend of the bride's Father. She smiled at this and enquired:

"How many children has he got?

I explained that he had four children which were three girls and a boy, and carrying on by saying that one of the other daughters was already married. I told her that his son was married before I became close enough to be invited to his wedding and his first daughter had married in a really conventional way with an Orthodox wedding ceremony which I had been lucky enough to attend. However, I remarked that although it had been a beautiful wedding, this one was too, but in a different way.

Analysis.

If you remember I knew the bride's Father, and in reality I do know this man. Yet even as I was dreaming this dream I was thinking that this could not be so because in real life my friend was a homosexual gentleman and had been aware of that all his life and indeed had been with the same partner for over thirty years. The fact that I was aware of this fact as the dream was unreeling means that I was also dreaming that I was dreaming. This is an exceptionally lucky concept to take place and it was happening which indicates once again that it is not only a premonition but a really good one and one that augers well for my future.

If you are keeping up with the story you will have already realised that if my friend is homosexual it is not likely that he would, be the Father of four children or any come to that. This is making the statement that things are not always as they appear to be and I need to look deeper. Because this friend connects to me in a work capacity, the situation that the premonition is about is a work related one. I told the lady that he had four children, which were one boy and three girls. The boy married and I did not attend. The first daughter had an Orthodox wedding; the second daughter had a beautiful but not such a regular wedding and this presumes that the third is to come.

This indicates to me that because I did not attend the boy's wedding something to do with my career went ahead blindly to get me started. The first girl having a big Orthodox wedding meant that I went about the next stage the right way and it went really well but there was something missing. This is portrayed by the fact that the third wedding was a special ceremony of a different kind that everyone was amazed by even though it was not conventional. This also meant that the third works-related thing to take place for me was to take me forward in leaps and bounds, which I would enjoy and would need to push a little on my own so that stage four indicated by the unmarried daughter would go really well for me and all involved.

Dream.
The lady went on to ask if the bride's Father was good at organising things and I told her that he was exceptionally good at it; She replied in answer to this:

"Oh good because I am told that John Inman is arranging things for you from Spirit where they will be organised to go well very quickly in the near future and that he was three times better at it than your friend,

132

the bride's Dad!"

Analysis

The lady who was a stranger to me asked if my friend was a good organiser to which I replied that he was really good at it, in fact he is an exceptional organiser. To which she replied:

"Oh good because I am told that John Inman was arranging things for you from Spirit where they will be organised to go well very quickly in the near future and that he was three times better at it than your friend, the bride's Dad."

They are telling me that important people in Spirit are now helping with the organising of my career and if I thought my friend was exceptionally good at this then I can expect help that is four times greater than I have received already, so therefore in the near future things will take off and go extremely well for me. Remember that three is a very lucky number and there were three female members of the story and as it changed from male (The Son) to female (the Daughters) Things began to improve with each stage this makes it clear that things will now go well for me. It happened at a time in my career pathway where I needed help and Guidance. I now know without doubt that I got it!

At this point I woke up from my dream and remembered it vividly. This was obviously a message from Spirit because of the way it had come through and the vividness of it.

DREAM 4
I dreamed that I woke up and sat up in bed to see that in the corner of my bedroom on the bedside table there was a mass of a white substance. As I strained my eyes to look at it closely I realised that it was Ectoplasm that I was seeing and as this realisation hit me, I became aware of many jets of light coming from and to the mass of ectoplasm, and could see a face smiling at me through the haze. It was at this point that I heard a very soft voice saying: "Jean, it is time." I was amazed by

this and suddenly realised that I was now awake and sitting up in bed watching the rays of light going back and forward from the ectoplasm, before it gently disappeared in front of my eyes and I knew that I had forgotten part of what had happened and no matter how hard I tried I could not recall it to my mind.

Analysis.

Whenever, a so called dream is not only vivid (which indicates that it is a message from Spirit) but is so real that the dreamer sleepwalks or at least sits upright in bed, it is a sign that things are about to happen in a new phase of the dreamer's life. However, the fact that in the beginning I was dreaming that I was sitting up in bed watching the jets of light and the ectoplasm when it was in fact happening at the same time, means great luck is about to come my way because I was in fact dreaming that I was dreaming which is a very auspicious sign. The soft voice is coming from someone I love in Spirit side. (I thought that you may be interested to know that it came from my sister Chris who is steadily watching my progress with great interest from the Spirit side of life.) She is letting me know that my time to go forward is here at last. Finding myself awake and still able to see the scenes that I saw in my sleep state, clearly defines that my dreams will come true because they are turning from a dream into reality; from being in my sleep to whilst I was awake.

Forgetting part of that dream and knowing that I had forgotten it, yet not being able to recall it, indicates the good that is about to happen, and because it has already been in my head once in the dream, I will recollect the situation. In other words I will get a distinct feeling of de'ja-vu when the time is right for the rest of the story to unfold.

Chapter Eleven
More Dreams

11
More Dreams

For three nights on the trot, I dreamed about new things to put in my dream cards that had not even entered my head. This was Spirit's way of offering me help at a time when they knew that I would not be too busy to listen.

Then the following night I had two dreams which I think you will find very interesting, so here they are broken down and analysed:

DREAM 1

Dream 1
I dreamed that Chris and I were due to go on stage in front of thousands of people to demonstrate our Mediumship.

Analysis:
This indicates: Chris who was only training at the time would develop enough to appear on stage in front of large audiences.

Dream:
In the dream just before we were due to go on stage I said to Chris", I must go for a quick wee before we are called". She, in a panicky voice retorted: "Jean you can't, there isn't time." My reply was: "Well okay but if I have to come off you will have to take over till I come back and they can't start without me can they?" She immediately changed her mind and told me to hurry up then. When I went into the door marked 'Ladies' I was shocked to find that there were no toilets in there at all, just wash basins and mirrors so I quickly returned backstage.

Analysis:
Meaning: It was telling me that even though I get extremely nervous before appearing on stage I should not worry because I will manage fine. This is defined by the fact that I wanted to go to the toilet yet when I could not find one I managed without. This tells me that it was only nerves telling me that I needed to go to the toilet, and I would manage without going.

Dream:
Chris came in and we were just about to leave to wait to be called back stage when I remembered that I had no lipstick on, so Chris hurriedly lent me hers and out we went. Once introduced, I lifted the curtain back and walked out to a massive applause and this is where I woke up.

Analysis:
Meaning: The fact that Chris loaned me the forgotten lipstick to appear on stage tells me that I will always be provided for, protected and seen for my ability and not what people say, so not to worry. Simple once it is worked out, isn't it?

In the second dream of that night:

DREAM 2

Dream:
My husband Mike and I were on our way somewhere in the car and just before we went over a hump backed bridge, Mike stopped the car and we got out. I cannot remember why we got out of the car so it obviously was not important, because we tend to remember the most vivid and important parts of our dreams.

Analysis:
Did you, whilst reading this, notice that we had stopped the car just before going over a humped back bridge? This meant that I was feeling as though I had got an obstacle to climb in my life and I was just about to approach that obstacle head on.

Dream:

I stood on the pavement which was only about eighteen inches wide and Mike was about to lift the boot of our car when suddenly we heard a very loud hoot of an owl and we both looked around towards the trees across the road where the noise had come from.

Analysis:

An Owl hooting from up high means that wise communication from high unseen places is coming my way. This is so because Owls are considered to be wise and he was hooting from high up and out of sight. Remember that hooting is an Owl's way of communicating.

Dream:

It was at this point that I saw a man standing about twelve feet away from us and also looking up at the trees. This meant that Mike was about four feet behind me and to my left and the stranger was approximately twelve feet in front of me to my right.

Analysis:

This was telling me that although I was surrounded by people; indicated by someone at each side of me but in different positions, I should listen to the wise communication from the sometimes unseen; Indicated by the fact that you can sometimes see Owls but we could not see this one.

Dream:

The leaves at the top of the tree started to move and a giant Tawny owl stepped into view on the top branch. He was around four feet tall and two feet wide. He was staring at me and his eyes were as big as tennis balls.

Analysis:

This says that the unseen are bigger and therefore wiser than I could ever imagine, and they were watching over me, even when I could not see them.

Dream:
Suddenly he took flight across the road over the privet hedge on our side of the road, flying off over the field. As he did so his shadow cast darkness over Mike and the stranger even though they were standing so far apart and Mike was in the road and the man on the path. Yet the sun came out and a ray of sunshine shone all over and around me.

Analysis:
The Owl flying away out of sight, but casting darkness over the two men present and letting the sun shine on and all around me, even though the two men were not standing together, tells me that even when out of sight they are protecting me from harm and lighting my way, so not to worry.

Dream:
After the owl had gone we expressed our amazement and went back towards the car to resume our journey. I was just about to climb back into my seat when I noticed that I had my slippers on and exclaimed to Mike "Oh God, have I got my shoes?" He answered "Yes I think so but it does not matter if you haven't because they will not care what you are wearing as long as you are there." At this point I woke up.

Analysis:
This part of the dream once again expresses that no matter how differently people try to portray me, through jealousy, it will not make any difference because my ability will shine through no matter what. Something that you may find strange also happened that night. I keep a book in which to write down my dreams on my bedside cabinet up against the wall and I usually place the television remotes on top of it after switching the television off before I go to sleep. I did this as normal but when I woke up after dreaming about the owl, my dream book was on the chair next to my bed. I should explain that I usually sit on this chair if I decide to write down my dreams in this book. I cannot honestly tell you whether I put the book on the chair in my sleep, ready to write in, or Spirit moved it there ready for me to write in, but either way it showed that Spirit were emphasising the importance of that

dream and its meaning, and making sure that I wrote its contents down so that I could follow the dream. This instantly meant that I thought it would be necessary to relate this true story to you so that you can see the strange and wonderful way in which Spirit work by correlating your sleep state dreams and your moments of being awake in life too.

It is now time for another exercise to develop your latent ability to link with your sixth sense. All you need for this is your pack of dream cards, a writing pad, a subdued light and a quiet room with a bed or couch to lie on comfortably.

1) First of all, lie down on your bed, preferably on your back, or in a position that you are most comfortable, yet you need to be lying in a way that you can see into the room easily.

2) Close your eyes loosely and gently smile.

3) Picture your body becoming weightless as though your body has become all floppy.

4) Whilst thinking happy thoughts and keeping your eyes closed, look towards the bridge of your nose with both eyes and keep a mental note of what you see.

5) After approximately thirty seconds gently open your eyes whilst trying to keep your body relaxed and floppy.

6) As you look across in front of you, you should be able to see a gentle fuzzy atmosphere across the other side of the room and you may feel a tingly sensation in your body.

   (The fuzziness you are seeing is because you have managed to change your vibration slightly and the tingling sensation is because you can now feel the Spirit World interacting with the magnets within your Auric field whilst trying to communicate with you.)

In case of confusion I should explain that your Auric field is a magnetic energy field all around your body's perimeter.

7) At this point you need to write down any results on your writing pad.

8) Take your dream cards out of their box and shuffle them, whilst trying to remain as floppy and relaxed as possible and thinking about the changed vibration.

   (This is important for the exercise because you are using the change of vibration that you have created to let the Spirit World know that you are asking for their direction.)

9) Holding the pack of cards in your right hand, lie back down, holding the cards so that they are face down on the bed where you are lying. (This means that the knuckles of your right hand will face towards the ceiling.)

10) Repeat numbers two to seven of the exercise.

11) Sit up and randomly spread your pack of dream cards out, Face down on the bed, without looking at them.

12) Sit up and randomly spread your pack of dream cards out, Face down on the bed, without looking at them.

13) Choose the two cards that you are most drawn to. (The rest of the pack can now be put away.)

14) Look at your two chosen cards and read their meanings in the little book that accompanies them.

15) Place them face up on your bed-side cabinet, or somewhere close to your bed where you sleep.

16) For three consecutive nights, look at your two cards before you settle down to sleep then repeat numbers one to four of the exercise until you fall asleep. This will indicate to your Guardian Angel that you wish them to communicate with you in your dreams.

17) All that is left to do now is to see whether your two cards and your dreams are compatible. (Sometimes it may look as though they are not but this is because you need to remember that as I said earlier, your dreams will be jumbled. The cards should help you to analyse your dream or dreams but if you need help with this then you can check out my web site and e-mail me, you will find the address in the back of this book.)

The more we practice this exercise the easier and more precise it will become. When I used my friend Chris as a guinea pig for this after being told by Mr R 'who is my Guardian Angel', that this would be a good way for people to practice changing their vibration', the first words out of her mouth, once she got over the shock that she had seen the vibration, and she had felt the tingling sensation were, "Well I cannot lie down and close my eyes to do this if I want to work in front of people can I?"

 And of course she is right and is not saying anything that I did not say myself in the beginning, but the easiest way to explain to you how this helps is to tell you that for any of you that drive or have driven a manual car, I am sure you will remember thinking to yourself, 'I will never be able to change gear and look out the front window at the same time!!' Yet in no time at all you find that you have driven to where you are going whilst thinking about other things and you do not even remember the journey. You automatically change gear and look through the front window without even thinking about it.

It is the same when it comes to changing your vibration. First you have to learn how? Then you have to practice until it becomes an automatic reaction. If you know me or you have read my two previous books you will know that people say that my catch phrase is:

'Do Not Think Whilst You Link.'

This is purely because thinking, just like love, where the Spirit World reside, changes everything. When learning to drive the car, you were thinking too much about what you were doing and not relaxing to cope with the matter in hand. This made it more difficult because it changed the way you reacted with your dexterity. When trying to alter our vibration, in the beginning the same theory applies, because when we are thinking about what we are trying to do we do not relax enough.

As I have already said, you need to practice going floppy; this serves to relax you down inside and starts to raise your vibration. Once you get used to doing this, you will suddenly find that you do not need to lie down, or close your eyes in order for this to happen. Just like driving the car it will happen naturally and automatically whenever the need arises for you to do so. This is simply because you will not be thinking about it anymore. So as I have said many times; do not think whilst you link!!!

Remember the old adage; practice makes perfect. Well this is definitely the case when linking with Spirit. By this I do not mean that anyone including myself can ever be one hundred percent perfect all the time, but it does mean that with practice you can perfect each step as you go along so that whilst you are needing to concentrate on the next step you are able to do so.

Chapter Twelve
Learning to Analyse Our Dreams

12
Learning to Analyse Our Dreams

This chapter is going to contain exercises that you will either find really easy or a little bit confusing. Therefore I am going to do my best to take you slowly by your thought process and guide you through it. First of all I would like to remind you that the closest thing to our ego is our name. This is why people are always impressed if we remember their name. Although linking to and with the Spirit World should never have anything to do with ego because if it does the Spirit World step back which means that if they do this, it becomes very difficult or even impossible to work out what they are trying to communicate to us, either for ourselves or for other people, thereby decreasing our ability as a Medium. I still feel that this is a good place to start because it is something that everyone can understand and relate to. I also keep asking you not to think whilst you link but in this case it is different because you do not have to work out what the communication is telling you personally; the Dream Cards will do this for you. I want you to sit somewhere where you will be totally comfortable and have no interruptions for this next exercise. You will once again need your pack of Dream Cards and a writing pad.

Write your name on a piece of paper out of your writing pad And place it somewhere at random between your pack of Dream Cards.

Close your eyes as you either sit or lie relaxed with your pack of Dream Cards clasped close to your chest with both hands around them.

Think clearly, my name is 'Jean' (but using your own name.) Can you please give me guidance on what I need to look for in my dreams over the next few nights?

Keep repeating this sentence over and over in your head whilst keeping your eyes shut.

Try to remember if you see, hear or sense anything at all during this process.

When you feel that the time is right, you can open your eyes. Although I must explain that you need to give yourself time to relax and change vibration before you are likely to see, hear or sense the Spirit World, unless of course you are already a trained Medium when it will happen naturally straight away. So I would advise giving it at least ten minutes or more for this part of the exercise.

Write down anything that you saw, heard, or sensed and do not forget to put the date at the top of your page because this may be very important later on.

Without disturbing the position of the cards in your pack, gently open them where the piece of paper with your name written on is situated. Read and write down the number and the sentence that are written on the cards on either side of your piece of paper.

Gently put the cards back in the same position as before but without the piece of paper.

Placing your Dream Cards face down, count down until you come to the number that coincides with the first letter of your name. For instance if your name is: Dawn you take the fourth card in the pile because the first letter of your name would be the fourth letter in the alphabet, as shown here:

Read the short sentence on the front of your chosen card and write it and the number written on your card down exactly as it is written, onto your writing pad.

Place the cards back onto the top of the pack where you have just taken them from.

Now repeat this process but this time using the first letter of your last name. If it happens to be the same card then the message will have double meaning, which will make it even more important.

Now I want you to place these cards back onto the pack of Dream Cards where they came from, then remove the top twenty six cards from your pack, putting them to one side.

You now have eighteen cards left in your pile out of the pack of forty four cards. Close your eyes and think of a number as quickly as you can.

Open your eyes and count down from the top of the remaining cards until you come to the number that you thought of. (If your number was higher than eighteen, start again at the top of the pack with the number nineteen until you reach the number that you thought of) Write the number and the sentence on this card onto your list.

You should now have a list of five cards and they should be written down like this example of my cards:

A) Card 11   EXPECT THE BEST.

You will receive what you expect to receive right now so expect the best

B) Card 18   GRACE.

Grace and serenity will take over your heart.

C): Card 9   DIVINE INTERVENTION.

All that you require can be achieved through divine intervention. Help is there for the asking.

D): Card 10
EXPECT THE BEST.

You will receive what you expect to receive right now so expect the best.

E): Card 21
IS IT SPIRIT!

Your next dream will be a message from the person you love most in the Spirit World. Act upon it.

Now you are ready to start reading your Dream Cards.

I know that once again this exercise may seem like a long drawn out process when you look at its length in this book but appearances can be deceptive and in this case they definitely are. It is also worth mentioning here that during the analysis of a dream or the interpretation of a communication from the Spirit World of any kind, appearances can also be deceptive.

Whilst analysing a dream we need to take all parts of that dream into consideration. This is why, that whilst dream dictionaries have their uses, people generally just take one aspect of the dream, like the fact that in the dream they were walking up the stairs. They look up this fact in their dream dictionary and conclude that this is what the dream means. Whereas, other aspects of the dream should be checked that turn it into a story.

For instance, walking up the stairs, on the face of it looks as if you are having an uphill struggle in life because you are required to climb up the stairs, which is always harder than going down. But if you add to the scenario the fact that you were lightly dressed in this dream and there was a light shining down the stairwell onto you, then the meaning changes. It is now saying that although it has been an uphill struggle of late, (depicted by climbing the stairs) things are now becoming easier (because you are wearing light clothing that makes it easier to move) and there is a light at the end of the tunnel showing good things to come are close by, (this is obviously shown by the light shining down the stairs onto you.) So you see things are never quite as simple as they appear. People also need to bear these rules in mind when interpreting a Spirit link. If you are thinking that I have forgotten about helping you to interpret your Dream Cards meanings, you are wrong. I just felt that the above information would help with this process. Let's read my five cards above:

Card A and card D were both:
EXPECT THE BEST.

You will receive what you expect to receive right now so expect the best.

As I pointed out to you before, if information of any kind is duplicated then you need to pay extra attention to it, as is the case when anything is duplicated in your life. This message was repeated twice so it is telling me to keep a positive outlook from beginning to end and everything bad will go away. I know that it means from beginning to end because it was my first card and my last but one card in the readings that were duplicated. This leaves one more card which is the "Is It Spirit" card indicating that Spirit are watching over me. The rest is easily calculated by the sentence written on the front of the card.

B) Card 18
GRACE.

Grace and serenity will take over your heart.

C) Card 9
DIVINE INTERVENTION.

All that you require can be achieved through divine intervention. Help is there for the asking.

E) Card 21
IS IT SPIRIT

Your next dream will be a message from the person you love most in the Spirit World. Act upon it.

These cards basically say that those that love me in Spirit are going to come forward in my dreams and bring all that I require so if I trust Spirit and expect the best in return I will get it. We know that it will be very soon because Spirit are going to guide me in my dreams and they would wait a while if it was meant for a long way off in the future.

So you see overall my card reading is telling me:

To keep a positive outlook from beginning to end and everything will go my way. Grace and Serenity will take over my heart so that all that I require can be achieved through divine intervention. Help is there for the asking. I should act upon my next dream as it will be a message from the person I love most in the Spirit World. That my life will become more peaceful with the difficulties in my life disappearing because I am being helped by unseen forces, which once again indicates that I have nothing to worry about. Spirit will Guide me through my dreams so that if I act upon their advice my dreams will come true very soon.

The full reading says:

The energies around you at this moment are exceptionally good but you will only get what you expect, so make the effort to expect the best and the effort will be made for the best to occur because things in your life at this minute can appear to be a bit heavy and a burden. Drawing the Grace card means that serenity will take over your heart and mind if you let it because Spirit will grace your dreams with their presence, thereby giving you the peace of mind to go forward. Therefore all that you require can be achieved through divine intervention. This help is yours for the asking so do not waste time procrastinating. Ask for help now, as your loved one is trying really hard to give you direction in your life. Please listen to your dreams then in effect you will be listening to the advice of the person you love most in the Spirit World. Listen to your next dream because it will indicate a way forward for you.

Once it is agreed by the person who is developing that the time is right for that person to start going forward, Spirit tend to pull out all the stops to help with this very important phase of their Development both during waking and sleeping hours. Here are some interesting ways in which they combine waking and sleeping time to help her to understand a few things which will help with her development and hopefully yours by reading about it. One day a few weeks ago whilst my friend Chris was at work and sitting at her desk, she was suddenly made aware of the fact that the telephone was ringing a number all by itself!! At that point some items of stationery and paperwork started to fall from her desk and she was reaching out in all directions trying to stop them from landing all over the floor, whilst at the same time picking up the telephone receiver to try and stop it dialling a number. At that moment Chris heard a voice at the other end of the telephone saying the name of her hairdresser's shop. This really puzzled Chris because she did not know the number without looking it up in her diary and the number was not in speed dial, or redial in the work's telephone memory either. Chris spoke to the lady on the other end of the telephone and she told her that the owner of the shop who is a close friend of Chris' was not at work today because she was not very well and she was also due to have an operation on her knee. Later that day Chris telephoned her friend to find that she was very poorly. This was her friend's Father letting Chris know that his Daughter needed her. Chris for her part remembers this occasion vividly and still to this day looks in wonderment at the way Spirit managed to communicate with her and in turn make her gain contact with her friend who was quite poorly at that time. Even a non-believer 'which Chris is not' would have to accept that these circumstances were odd and that maybe there was an outside influence involved, as there certainly was in my opinion. Remember that this incident happened for real whilst Chris was awake and at work and as the phone number physically rang her friend's number for her when it was not in the telephone memory, it could not have been imagination could it?

Not long after this incident took place and definitely heightened Chris' senses to the Spirit side of life, she woke up suddenly one night to find herself standing by her bedroom door next to the light switch, when she had been in bed and did not know how she got there other than the fact that she had probably been sleep walking. She saw something move out of the corner of her eye and looked up to where the light bulb was in the centre of the ceiling to see a huge spider the size of her hand hanging on its thread from the light shade above her bed. She switched the light on to find that it had gone. It was in fact, only a Spirit Spider. I can actually feel the fear building up in any person who is reading this and suffers from arachnophobia, but you need not worry. Spirit indicated that she should look up to see the spider above her bed where she had been sleeping so that she would see this gigantic creature and know that if it had been a real life over grown insect and not a Spirit one she would surely have been in a lot of danger if she had stayed in bed asleep!! However, they had managed to bring her safely out of bed to the light switch so that she would be able to see the situation that was taking place. This means that Spirit are telling her that they will protect her from any danger and see that she is where she needs to be at any given time so that she can have the best advantages in life and with her work with Spirit. Therefore she has no need to worry. I would like you to be aware that this second event took place both during sleeping and being awake because she definitely remembers being in bed and cannot recall getting out of bed and walking over to the light switch. She therefore was obviously sleep-walking to get over to the light switch whilst still in sleep state. Those who know me or have read my previous books will know that I have been known to sleep walk a lot in my life span so far and this is a classic case of someone who is very Psychic and Spiritually aware being alerted to the fact that they can communicate with Spirit whilst in sleep state and that they can carry this gift forward into their waking life.

Spirits were talking to her whilst she was still in sleep state. They sometimes do this, almost as if they are relaying a story to you which I feel was the case on this particular occasion. Because your Spiritual awareness is becoming very alert, the story and events being relayed appear to be real as if they are really happening to the person who is experiencing the dream/ Spirit conversation at that time. It is therefore, not surprising that you start to act out the things that you are being told, just as Chris got out of her bed to switch on the light so that she could see the spider hanging from the light bulb. I would like to say here that if you come across someone who is either out of bed or throwing themselves around in bed yet still asleep, you should tell them to either go back to bed or settle down to sleep using a firm, loud voice without touching that person harshly, as you do so. If you do this the person will follow your instructions, because to them you will become part of that dream and the scenario being acted out. This is safe and always works. If however you touch that person suddenly you cause the equivalent of a shock wave to their system through the magnetic effect of their Aura making them feel that you are part of the danger and the dream they already feel they are part of. This can in turn cause them to lash out, run, or indeed go into shock; putting them in danger. It is therefore far safer to speak to the person firmly but calmly. She was meant to wake up whilst by the light switch so that she would definitely remember the dream/incident taking place, which she does. When she looked up to see the huge spider after switching on the light, she had woken up but was still in a slightly altered state of consciousness, which is how a Medium is when linking to and with the Spirit World. She could therefore see what Spirit was showing her clearly. However, once she moved towards the light to take a closer look she would naturally alter her state of consciousness back to normal by the sudden movement. Therefore the spider that was in Spirit and part of the story and lesson she was being shown disappeared, or at least she could no longer see it. Once fully trained, a Medium can move about without altering their state of consciousness up and down, so they no longer lose their link to Spirit because of this.

Spirit had now correctly introduced Chris to the fact that they could talk to her whilst she was asleep, so the next step was to use this faculty to introduce her to her Guardian Angel/Main Guide. This is when she had this dream:

DREAM 1:
One day after Chris had sorted out the telephone wires at the bottom of the stairs leading up to her flat, she climbed back up the staircase and as she turned the corner towards the second flight of stairs she saw a man standing at the top on her landing. The man was looking down at her as she climbed the stairs towards him. He was wearing a long coat which was gold/yellow and black in colour, although there was more gold/yellow than black. The coat appeared to be covered in little square shapes. Most of these squares were gold/yellow with a black border but there was also an occasional totally black square. The coat included a wide black belt or sash, which was tied neatly around his waist with no ends hanging down. As she looked towards him she could see that he was about 5'11" in height and aged approximately 76 years old.

Analysis:
The man was wearing that beautiful coat which almost acted as though they were his medals. The reason for the coat being covered in squares of the same size means that in life we tend to think that some problems are bigger than others and therefore insurmountable. In reality though this is not true, they just appear that way. The squares are equal in size and tell us that when analysed they are all the same size as each other. The yellow gold colour means that her Guardian Angel has injected the very best into her life should she wish to use it. It is the colour of high Spirit. The black borders around each square say that even when things are going really well you always need to be aware that there is a slightly troublesome area in the background which you need to be both aware of and keep on top of. The occasionally completely black square signifies that at times you will need to experience the bad times, but remember it is surrounded in yellow/gold squares which are the good things about to take place.

Dream:

At that point the man held out a few items to show her, amongst which, were a telephone, an answering machine complete with its instruction booklet and some money. He asked her which she thought should go first if she had to put them in order of importance, with the most important item placed first. Before she could answer this he asked if she thought money was the most important item? Without hesitation she replied no, that although money was important she felt that the telephone was the most important one to her. As she said this she asked the man his name and he replied Fruteros or something similar that she could not quite understand, but before she could remark further he said "You can call me Mr A. I come from India." Although he comes from India he was not dark skinned in the slightest, but of English appearance. He went on to tell her that his name is: Fruteros Augustus Archibaldus, or Mr A. He is Chris' Guardian Angel. Nice introduction don't you think? The fact that Mr A was wearing this coat when he introduced himself to Chris says that she need not worry because he is there always surrounding her with good vibrations even when things appear to be bad. The operative words here are 'appear to be!!!'

Analysis:

The list of items and their order of appearance were forgotten as she got caught up asking about him. Unfortunately she woke up before she could get back to that subject but she felt that she had learned a lot just the same. This is quite often how Spirit will portray information to you, especially if you are not yet fully capable of connecting to them whilst you are awake yet. It is always important to give credence to the fact that we need to get things into perspective and I would agree with Chris that money is important because we cannot live without it but never the most important aspect. Yet I would also agree that a telephone is a means of communication and from my point of view, communication is the very best gift that we have in whatever way we use it. Mr A obviously agreed with this to allow the dream communication to finish before she had sorted out the items. They were not really important, the introduction to him and his protection were the main reason for the dream and his visit. Remember they were also indicating that she was protected in the sleep walking scenario with the spider. Can you see a pattern forming?

DREAM 2:
In this dream there was a field full of buttercups or dandelion flowers (Chris was not certain which but they were definitely yellow flowers) with a fence all around the perimeter. She saw a swarm of buttercup and dandelion heads going past all around this scene, (in other words lying around the field like a swarm of bees.) There were strips of golden light all around.

Analysis:
First of all I should say that the golden yellow colour that was predicted by the buttercups/dandelions is a colour for teaching or learning from high Spirit. (Remember the coat in the last dream!!)

If we look at the fact that the field perimeter was surrounded by a protective fence, it is saying once again that the protection is all around her whilst she is learning. (It is protection once again.) The strips of Golden light being all around say that the protection is from God and high Spirit. (MR A.)

Dream:
There was a nearly new building, (which was noticeable by the new bricks that it was built with) There was a sign hanging above the door which said in clear words:

DANCE

MUSIC

MEDIUMSHIP

The word Mediumship was in noticeably larger writing than the words Dance and Music. Chris also had the feeling with this that I owned the building and not that it was advertising someone about to appear there.

Analysis:

As for the brand new building belonging to me and saying the above sign, with the top two words, Dance and Music being smaller than the word Mediumship, it is literally telling her that she has been involved in Dance and then Music through those special people whom she loves, but now the link with Mediumship is for her personally with my Guidance. It is with my Guidance because if you remember she said that she felt that the building belonged to me, therefore this indicates that I will be helping her to develop spiritually. The building is new because it is only over recent years that she has decided to develop her Spiritual gifts, and has now already started to do so with my Guidance. Can you see that Chris' dreams are taking her forward on her Spiritual and physical life pathway? She is being told all kinds of information that will help her along her way.

DREAM 3:

In this dream Chris was driving her car, with her Mother seated next to her in the passenger seat. There was a car in front of them as she drove along a road that had large old houses on each side. Suddenly and without warning a car reversed out of one of the drives attached to the houses into the pathway of the car in front of hers, causing the driver to brake suddenly. Although he hit the car it was only a slight collision.

Analysis.

First of all Chris was driving along with her Mum in the car so she was safe because she is a good and careful driver and is close to her Mother who is one of the nicest ladies that you could wish to meet. The two of them enjoy a very close relationship and they often go on trips in the car so this dream was touching normality. It also indicates that she is not alone, that people who love her and whom she loves are always near at hand, A car reversed out suddenly causing both Chris and the driver of the car in front to brake with little warning. This is pointing out that as in life where problems can project into our lives seemingly from nowhere, Spirit can appear with little or no warning to give a message to the recipient here, to help with any given situation, therefore things are not usually as bad as they would seem.

Dream:
The car in front was driven by a young woman and although Chris could not see her face, she knew that it was a daughter of a lady who had worked with her many years earlier. She could see that the driver of the car that had reversed in front of her was a stockily built man with dark hair and moustache, wearing an Arran jumper. Although she felt that she knew this man, she could not place him at the time. It was not until later that day that she realised that he reminded her of someone she knows in America.

Analysis:
The driver of the car in front, being the daughter of a woman whom she used to work with and the fact that the car was in front of her and not behind indicates that those in our past are also in our future. In other words it is saying that those we have loved but are in our past because they have gone to Spirit or away from our lives, are also here walking ahead of us to protect us from harm, and are indeed part of our present and our future. She did not recognise the man who had reversed out of his drive at the time but later was able to work out who he was. This was saying that sometimes people who we know very well come to visit us from Spirit but we sometimes find it difficult to know who they are until we have gained more information, which in the dream Chris did by going away, being more relaxed and thinking about it. In other words it is telling you to relax with the information that you receive and it will come to you more easily who is there.

Dream:
She suddenly became aware that she was now out of her car and looking through one of their car windows where they were both sitting talking. The two people then came to an agreement about the accident. They decided that neither of them would do anything about the accident because they felt that it was neither of their individual faults. The one car should not have reversed into her but she had driven into the back of his car which would shift the blame to her. Chris went back to her car and told her Mum that it was okay because the two drivers were not going to do anything about it but have settled it

amongst themselves. Once back at her Mother's house a friend called Jen was there and Chris explained it all again and asked if they both knew why they were both at fault, but neither of them could say, so she explained that, as I said before, one car should not have been reversing onto a main road and the other driver should have left enough space to brake on time in order not to hit anything that comes out in front of her, because she had gone into the back of him.

Analysis:

These two people coming together to discuss the way forward is saying that if she asks Spirit they will call for the help of others to help her to understand. This is also depicted by the fact that once they did this they were able to sort the problem out amicably where they were both happy. So you see if you ask Spirit for help they will make it so that both yourself and the recipient of the message are happy. Chris explaining things to her Mum and her friend once back at her Mother's home, because they did not know the answer, tells her that one day in the future she will not only link well to Spirit and in doing so help people here, but she will also teach Spirit linking too. Both her Mum and her friend are also developing, which gave rise to this part of the dream being involved. Again as in a previous dream the message is being given that things are not always as bad as they appear to be at first sight, and that although Chris always has the company of those she loves she can cope on her own if she needs to. This is depicted by the bump only being a slight one and the people involved sorting the problem out amongst them-selves without any major catastrophe taking place or needing outside help after all, and Chris being able to explain it all to her Mother and friend.

DREAM 5:

This is one dream that really puzzled Chris. It was one where she saw herself coming out of the Medium's room (in one of the local Spiritualist Churches) to go and sit down in the congregation. She said that she could not see myself and Mike in the room but she was sure we were in there. The Church was totally empty except for the Chairperson who was with Chris as they walked into the Church. She said that she knew the chairperson was with her although she could not see the person, just as she could not see Mike or myself.

Analysis.

Chris was at first aware of coming out of the Medium's room and entering the Church with the Chairperson whom she could not see and that she was also aware of myself and Mike being in the Medium's room although again she could not see us. This was telling her that she would in the future be working for Spirit in her own right and although she would be aware that Mike and I were there to give support she would not really need us as she would be capable of going it alone. The fact that she could not see the Chairperson even though she knew that that person was there with her says that she will be working in many different Churches and venues because there will be a different Chairperson at each event, so it does not matter who that person is because they will be different at each place she works, but that Chairperson will definitely be there because she will be working the circuit as a Medium in her own right.

Dream:

She was looking at the chairs which were at that time empty, and noticed that they were all the same except for one chair in the middle row situated centrally in that row. This particular chair had a beautiful tapestry back instead of the plain one that the rest of the chairs in the room had. As she looked at this chair it was noticeable that the bottom edge of this tapestry back was frayed and had not been stitched, even though the edge was totally straight. It was then that she realised that there was no actual seat to this chair, only a back which was joined to the two adjacent chairs on either side. Therefore instead of a space between the two chairs the gap was blocked by this tapestry backing.

Analysis:

Seeing a room full of empty chairs, connected by this beautiful tapestry chair back in the centre, was indicating that although it was not clear to her at the moment, she will have really good congregations to listen to her working. The fact that the bottom of the tapestry was a perfect straight line but was unstitched and frayed along the edge was saying that her work with the public will go far but her pathway towards learning is not yet complete, but going really well to plan and just needs the finishing touches before they can move her forward.

I hope you are beginning to understand how Spirit can bring messages to us in our dreams during sleep state in order to give us direction and or guidance with whatever situation we are dealing with in our lives at that particular time. They sometimes even use this method with Mediums such as myself yet they can quite easily talk to me or other Mediums whilst awake. This is because in the hustle and bustle of their very busy lives, Mediums can be the worse culprits for not listening to what Spirit are telling them for themselves because they are too busy obtaining information for other people. However if Spirit talk to them in their dreams they have a tendency to sit up and take notice of what they are being told.

Chapter Thirteen
Misunderstandings

13

Misunderstandings

My daughter Toni has a lot of ability where linking to the Spirit world is concerned yet she is very afraid of them just the same. In September 2005 she moved house into an old property where there would be plenty of space for her two children to grow. The children at this time were Georgina who was two years old and Thomas nearly three months. One day she telephoned me and told me in a voice full of horror that she needed me to go and check out her house because it was haunted. I laughed as I enquired what had happened to make her jump to this conclusion. She quickly explained that she had been upstairs and about to put some teething gel onto Thomas' gums before he went to sleep when the telephone rang downstairs. Placing the teething gel on a ledge she ran down to answer the call but on her return found that the teething gel was missing and was nowhere to be seen. She went into Georgina's room to check that she had not managed to climb out of her cot but she was fast asleep. Returning to the room she searched for the gel but to no avail, it was still nowhere to be seen.

After a while Toni noticed that Thomas was now asleep and therefore did not need his gums to be soothed anyway. She went back down the stairs feeling very confused about the whole episode but soon got interested in the television and put it out of her mind. That is until the following day when after taking Georgina to nursery and settling Thomas for his morning sleep she went about the tasks of the day.

Finishing the housework that needed doing downstairs she checked Thomas before heading upstairs. She tidied her own bedroom and Georgina's then Thomas'. As she finished, once again the telephone rang out, she gave Thomas' bedclothes one last smooth with her hand before racing down the stairs to answer the telephone before it woke the baby up. Later that evening when she was about to place Thomas in his cot she noticed a strange looking lump in the bedclothes so curiously felt the space only to find that the lump in question appeared to be hard. Toni stripped the bed right down to the mattress before discovering that the missing teething gel from the night before had been placed almost ceremoniously under the sheets near to where Thomas' head would be. I told her not to worry they would not hurt her and promised that I would call round to her home as soon as I could to sort it out for her.

The following day Toni telephoned me once again but appeared even more alarmed than she had done the day before. She blurted out: "Mum, you must come and get **your** hoolie goolies out of my house. (This is Toni's pet name for Spirits.)

I laughed as I asked why she thought they were mine adding that just because I am a Medium does not mean that I am responsible for all Spirits. However, she said that the house was okay before I visited, the day after she moved in so therefore she thought that I must have left the Spirit there. I explained to her that I did not go around taking Spirits and leaving them everywhere I go and pointed out that maybe she had not lived there long enough to notice them before my visit. She laughed and said:

"Well you can still take them away".

With this I asked what had happened now?

She explained that to start off with she heard footsteps running across the bedroom floor and had rushed upstairs to tell Georgina off for being out of bed but when she got there, once again she was fast asleep!! She cautiously checked all the rooms then returned downstairs to where Thomas was sleeping soundly. Then she heard a baby crying upstairs through the baby monitor yet once again both children were fast asleep.

A few minutes later Toni took the baby up to bed but was shocked to find that the very tidy cot had been disturbed and there was a dip in the sheets as if a child had been lying there!! Once again poor Georgina was checked and found to be innocent. Then the following day Georgina was sitting on the armchair watching television and Thomas was tucked onto the corner of the settee.

Toni popped into the kitchen which was only the next room, clicked the kettle on and returned to the children. As she did so she could hear both children laughing and found Thomas lying on the carpet in the centre of the lounge and Georgina sitting next to him where they were both laughing away merrily.

I would like to point out that not only was Georgina just two but she was a small two and there is no way that she could move the baby without hurting him because she would need to drag him off the settee. Toni checked him over and he was fine, I do not know what you would make of that but I know what my instant opinion was.

It is always worth remembering that for someone who resides on the Spirit side of life, there is no need to physically lift anything or anybody. This is because, as I have said before, everything and everybody is made up of molecules and all the Spirit would have to do is dematerialise the sofa where Thomas was lying, (In other words make it disappear for a split second) then re-materialise it, (make it come back) when Thomas was on the floor and able to roll and play. I should make you aware here that Spirit only come in love so therefore they would never place Thomas or anyone else in a position of danger.

If they had, then Thomas' Guardian Angel would have alerted his Mum, as they did.

It is amazing how people assume things that cause confusion about how Spirit work to bring communication to us from the other side. Only a few days ago my daughter came along to a Town Hall event where I was appearing and bought my nine year old Granddaughter Leah along to see me. Once they were on their way home after the event, Leah said to her Mum:

"I am really proud of my Nanny you know Mum".

To which Dawn replied:

"Really darling, why is that?"

"Because she is famous and all those people came just to see my Nanny."

Dawn laughed and Leah continued:

"How does Nanny know all those things about them people? Do they tell Nanny before she goes on stage?"

Dawn assured her that this was not the case and she retorted:

"Do the Ghosts tell her then?"

My daughter assured her that this was the case but said that they liked to be called Spirits and not Ghosts. My Granddaughter who can be very quick in her thinking replied:

"No they don't like you to call them Ghosts because this can be a bit scary for people and Spirits are not scary are they?"

Whilst I am really pleased that my Granddaughter is proud of me and how hard I work for Spirit. To a nine year old, I suppose it does look impressive that a large hall is full of people who have come supposedly to see the person on stage!!

However, the truth of the matter is that these people really come in the hopes of having an audience with the people whom they love who have passed on to the Spirit World. For this to take place it is obviously important that the Medium knows what they are doing so are therefore linking to Spirit well enough for the information to be clear.

Meaning that from this point of view, yes they do come to see me. But in truth any Medium who does the job well would suit the audience. In other words it is not me that is famous but the connection to another World that brings hope of the existence of life after death and therefore a belief in the fact that we or our loved ones are not lost forever once we have left our earthly body.

Leah is right though when she says that people are more afraid when we use the word Ghost than if we use the word Spirit. This is because the word Ghost conjures up all sorts of thoughts in the head, whereas the word Spirit seems to have very different connotations altogether.

The English language itself does not help where this is concerned because of common phrases that use these two words. For instance I am sure that we have all heard of these expressions:

'He or she has not got a Ghost of a chance of achieving that.'

In other words what they are trying to do is more or less out of sight and therefore not really possible!!

'He or she looks Ghostly white.'

Which means that the person being spoken about does not look at all well?

We know that a 'Ghost writer' works very hard but does not get much of the appreciation for the book or whatever they are Ghost writing. Yet if we look for phrases where the word, Spirit is indicated, they usually have good meanings. For instance:

'He or she is in good spirits'

This indicates that the person we are talking about is happy.

When someone is cheerful in the face of adversity, they are said to be keeping up their spirits. People always comment on these occasions:

"That's the spirit."

A spirit level makes sure that something is straight and therefore right. It acts almost like an invisible guide to get it right.

If we talk about spiriting something away, it usually means that we can make the bad things disappear.

There are of course many other examples and naturally if you look hard enough you can find examples of the opposite but generally it is this way round.

Chapter Fourteen
Developing Students

14
Developing Students

Helping students to develop can be a mixture of fun, laughter and hard work. The hard work mostly comes about when it is time to try and convince a student that the time is right for them to be on the rostrum or stage in front of people so that they can get some practice at this and help calm their nerves for when in the future it is time for them to link to Spirit from that position. Those who read my first book will probably remember how a student and good friend of mine named Sue, shook so much that she could hardly breath, when she managed to inadvertently trick herself into helping me to get her invited to work alongside me as my student on the rostrum of a lovely Spiritualist Church in Shrewsbury. She did brilliantly well even though she shook so much that the stage was rattling just like it did when I made my de'bu't on a rostrum for the first time in Catshill Bromsgrove.

Well this year it was Chris' turn to tremble. She has been developing, and had improved a great deal but like all students she did not feel that it was time to face an audience of living people yet!! I however, had a different point of view about this. (I find it very interesting that students start off nervous about talking to the so-called dead and end up nervous of talking to the living. Although it has to be said that from a Medium's point of view I think talking to Spirit can be invariably easier than talking to people in the here and now!!!) I had at first persuaded Chris to present me on stage so that she could get used to what to do, and not do, when talking to an audience and although she was nervous this went really well. A couple of weeks later she was driving me to a venue in Newtown Wales when we stopped half way there for a cup of coffee. Whilst having our drink Chris remarked to me that she was not ready to link on the rostrum yet. I grinned and asked her where that had come from? (What do you think? I think that maybe it was a quick psychic flash!!!)

She told me that she remembered that the first place where Mike had given a link from Spirit to a congregation was at Newtown Church and she was not ready to do that yet. This made me laugh as I answered "Nervous aren't we? What makes you think that I will get you up to link? I have not said anything YET" This reply made Chris really nervous and she said "Jean you have to promise me that you will not get me up to link on the rostrum tonight" I laughed at this and we bantered back and forward on the subject for several minutes before I promised her that I would not make her do a link to Spirit in front of the congregation that night. Anyone who knows me well would know that I never break promises once I have made them where at all possible.

Chris relaxed with a sigh of relief and we resumed our journey. Once there the Chairperson told me that she had stepped in at the last minute because the original chairperson was ill and she had only just found a reading so I replied "I am sure that Chris will do the reading for you if you ask her to." The look of horror on Chris' face was really obvious as she retorted straight away. "No, I can't do it!" I of course came back straight away with, "Yes you can, you want to help this lady out don't you, and it is only a reading, you can manage that?" Chris however, was adamant that she could not do this and we bantered back and forward a few times before the chairlady said, "Don't worry I will do it." My immediate reply was that surely she did not want the lady to do everything herself!! With this Chris agreed to do the reading just as I knew she would. Next we had to make a decision about which reading she would recite. The chairperson was really pleased that Chris had agreed to do the reading part of the service for her because this allowed her to concentrate on the job at hand of chairing. She handed Chris an open book on the page of her chosen reading for that evening. After looking at this she was horrified and retorted "I can't do this one, it is too long. I thought the reading was usually short." We both laughed in response to this as I quickly tried to reassure her that she could do it, and it would be okay but she only answered: "Readings are normally short. A few lines long, this one has three pages. I explained that it does not matter how long the reading is because you are drawn to that particular reading because Spirit realise that it will help someone who will be in the congregation that evening. She, however, still thought that it was too long for her to read and expressed this opinion strongly as it went back and forward in discussion between us.

By this time the chairlady had begun to feel really sorry for Chris and said that it would be okay if she changed the reading for a smaller one. I noticed the excited expression as this prospect came across Chris' face so quickly remarked: "Yes you can but remember that Spirit will have drawn the lady to that reading because it has something in it to help someone who will be in the Congregation tonight, but if you still want to change it go ahead, it will be alright." I knew that once again this would reach out to Chris' better nature and she would agree to comply with our wishes and read the longer reading after all, and she did. At this everyone would be happy including Chris once the reading was over and she could see that it went well and she could do it. At this she, without hesitation replied, "Okay you win I will read this one!"

Once it was Chris' turn to stand up, she was very obviously nervous to me because I knew her well, yet the congregation said afterwards not only how well she had done, but they could not see much sign of the nerves she was feeling. As she rose to her feet I whispered not to worry because her Guides, her loved ones in Spirit and I were close to give support. She gave a semi smile and off she went to read a perfect reading. As she did so I noticed that Chris' dog that is in Spirit came close up to her legs to bring support. This may not seem much if you are not a dog lover but to Chris it would be and was very important.

She not only read the chosen reading but made a superb job of it and the chairlady told her afterwards that there was a little dog standing next to her all the time that she was reading. When she described the dog it was Chris' much loved and missed dog Dougal in the Spirit world. Chris of course was delighted and said that she did feel something around her legs but did not know what it was so put it down to be being a draught. I assured her that it was not a draught but it was in fact Dougal visiting for moral support. This really pleased her because of the fact that it meant that he was there to give her that much needed support.

As soon as the service had finished people started to come forward to speak to us as they usually do after a service. A gentleman told Chris that something in the reading was very important to him and connected to someone he loved in the Spirit World, adding that it had made him feel as though he had received a message from his loved one in Spirit which he very much needed at that time. I smiled in Chris' direction and simply said one word with a knowing grin, "See!" She had to admit that she was glad that she had decided to stick with the original choice of reading and not only because it had helped the man although this was obviously the most important aspect, but because she now knew that she could do it. That was the first time for her to get used to facing an audience for more than a presenting purpose and she passed the test with flying colours. All's well that ends well don't you think, and Chris was one step closer to having the confidence to trust herself in front of an audience, because it is not Spirit that people do not trust on these occasions, it is themselves.

As for me, my tactics had obviously appealed to Chris' wonderful better nature and she had agreed even though at first it was against her better judgement. I smiled smugly to myself because I had managed to get her up in front of the people that evening without breaking my promise. 'After all she was not linking to Spirit was she?' I always try to make students aware that if you are asking Spirit for anything then you have to be precise because Spirit interprets exactly what you say, as you say it. I work for Spirit everyday of my life because it is a lifetime commitment as far as I am concerned. Therefore, the same rule applies when you are talking with me.

Only one week later we were on our way to a lovely Spiritualist Church in Gloucester where I had been booked to hold the Divine service.

Whilst we were on the way to Church Chris commented to me with a huge smile on her face that she would be safe today because it was my first time demonstrating at this particular Church and she knew that I would never ask to take a student on when I had not worked there before. She is right about that. However, shortly after we arrived at the Church we were sitting in the little room provided for the Medium having a cup of coffee when the president's wife asked me if I had brought a reading with me. I said no I had not because the Medium does not have to bring a reading when visiting most Churches, therefore I did not realise that it would be required of me.

To this she responded with: "Well there are a lot of books on the bookshelf that you could choose a reading from, or I could read one for you." Before I had the chance to answer she said: "Or this young lady could read for us out of one of your books", pointing to Chris as she did so. I answered quickly before Chris could have the chance to think about it and say no, "Yes that is a good idea." Chris' mouth fell open and before she could say anything the President's wife trundled off to put an extra chair for Chris on the Rostrum. Although complaining at first, she told me afterwards that it was a good experience because after she had done her reading and got over her nerves, she could settle down and watch the expressions on people's faces as they received and understood their messages. All good students need a push forward when it is time, but it is purely their lack of confidence that is stopping them.

I am now going to suggest another exercise that will help with your confidence. All you will need for this is a pack of my Dream Cards, a notepad and pen, (which should be kept close to your bed) and a comfortable place to sit, either on or near to your bed. Just before you retire I want you to get ready for bed then sit and make yourself comfortable either on or near to your bed, taking the Dream cards out of the pack and holding them against your chest with the pictures facing towards you. Spread them out towards your chest in a fan shape as much as is comfortable without altering your ability to relax because this relaxation is essential at this point in the exercise. Now I want you to think of something happening within your life that you need guidance with. I suggest that the first time that you try this it is better to think of a small factor and not a really large and major problem.

For instance should I buy a certain pair of shoes that I have taken a liking to in the shoe shop window?

'I must say here that it is not a good idea to get used to asking for Spirit's help and guidance with everything in your life. You have personal responsibility to make your own decisions because then you learn the lessons in life that you are here to learn and Spirit cannot take that away from you because it is an essential part of your destiny. However, for these exercises it will be alright to use this as a way forward to you interpreting your own dreams.'

Close your eyes and think very clearly of the occurrence that you need the Spirit World's guidance with, whilst still holding your Dream Cards against your chest. After one or two minutes open your eyes and lifting your cards away from your chest, fan them out face down on the bed. Closing your eyes once more think very clearly, 'which card should I choose to help with my decision?' After a few seconds open your eyes and the card that you are drawn to is the card that you will need. I must add however, that on occasions you may be drawn to two cards. If this is the case you should pick them both up because it is guidance from Spirit that you will need more than one. Look at any words displayed on your card or cards, trying to memorise as much about it as possible.

Now I want you to place the chosen card or cards face up, flat on your bedside cabinet or somewhere close to where you will be sleeping. If there are two cards, place them next to one another so that they are not touching. This is purely because if the cards are touching one another in any way it will serve to confuse the answer that you are seeking.

Forgetting the card for a moment, go about the business of finishing getting ready for bed. Then once you are in bed and snuggled down in the normal way that you sleep, I want you to try to picture the contents of your card or cards in your head. Keep doing this until you fall to sleep. If during the course of this part of the exercise your mind starts to wander to other things that are happening in your life at the time do not worry about this, but as soon as you realise what is happening go back to the contents of your chosen card or cards. This is quite normal because it is impossible to empty our mind entirely without special training.

When you wake up in the morning it is important to write down in a notepad kept especially for this purpose, exactly what if anything that you remember of any dreams that you had during sleep state. Still write it down if you did not dream at all because there is even a reason for this! This may seem tedious but I am asking you to repeat this exercise every night for three consecutive nights in a row. This is still the case even if you feel that your first night revealed your answer. This is because it is not always as straight forward as you would think to analyse a dream and it is important to look for repetitive actions or pieces of information. If something keeps recurring repetitively in your life it is because your Guardian Angel is trying to tell you something and this is also the case in your dreams.

Once all three nights are written down in your notepad, it is time to make a list on a fresh page of each thing that occurred within these dreams. If for instance you were asking about the shoes in our example and you saw the shoe shop locked three or more times then Spirit are saying that you should not get these shoes because it is not in your best interest to do so. If however, you saw the shop locked once but open throughout the rest of the dreams then they are saying that you should wait a while before purchasing these shoes. The shop always being open is obviously giving you the go ahead to purchase the shoes. If the shoe shop does not appear in your dream at all then you need to work out how your new shoes could possibly have any connection to what your dreams were saying, after which you should work out a connection whilst remembering that our brain dreams back to front and upside down and during this process they become jumbled. For instance if the dream was portraying that you were in need of protection in any way then your new shoes would protect your feet, so therefore it is a yes. If the dream was indicating that you were vulnerable right now, then you should wait before contemplating buying new shoes. If the dream was portraying you happy with your lot in life then it is okay to buy those shoes because the time is right to have what you want. I can assure you that with practice it becomes much easier to interpret your own dreams or anyone else's come to that.

You are probably thinking at this moment in time, what has all this got to do with either gaining confidence or linking to Spirit for that matter? Well the answer is; it helps with your confidence because it puts you in a position where you have to work out the answers for yourself without any external help apart from that of the Spirit World. It helps with learning to link with the Spirit World because when most students begin to practice to use their Spiritual Gifts they are mainly aware of their Clairsentient abilities, which as I have said in my previous books, means clear sensing abilities. It always makes me smile when I think that Clairsentience means clear sensing because from my experience when you first start to practice using this ability it is anything but clear!! This is purely because it is human nature to try to work things out, when in fact whilst using this ability it is best to bear in mind my catchphrase which is 'Do not think whilst you link.' In other words when the Spirit World express a fact like they do when they are putting something on our senses, it is important to express that fact exactly as it is given, because if you do not do this then the meaning of the message will be changed totally, thereby rendering it impossible to understand.

The same can be said of dream communication from the Spirit World because they are in fact using our senses during our dream state to express their communication to us. This is so because whilst we are asleep and dreaming our brain turns the dream around to change it into word form in the hopes that we will understand its meaning. This is the same as we do when we are awake and thinking. For instance: 'If Spirit put onto your senses that the man in Spirit and the man who the communication is for are rolling on the floor with their arms around each other as if they were in the midst of a struggle, it would be easy to think about it and say that they did not get on and were always fighting with one another! When in fact, the two men were really close, and used to play fight. But because you did not explain to the recipient of the message how you came to the conclusion that they were always fighting then the real meaning will never be reached, thereby causing disillusion and non belief in what was really a very accurate message from Spirit. Dreams are the same because when our brain attempts to turn the dream into a story, it changes the real message just as if we are thinking, which is exactly what our brain is doing to work out our dream even though we are asleep at the time. Unfortunately, we do not have the luxury of not thinking whilst we link during our sleep state because our brain does it naturally. In other words we are not in control of our brain whilst asleep as we can be when awake. Therefore, the dream is naturally muddled up and needs interpreting, because the thinking has already subconsciously taken place, whereas, with a link from Spirit whilst we are awake and in full control of our faculties, we have the choice whether we change it and jumble it up or not.

It is time to get back to using your dream cards. I now think that we should practice using the chosen card or cards from before whilst we are still awake and in control of what we think. If it is at all possible I would like you to either invite a couple of friends around to your home or go out and visit a couple of friends at their home. Although I must add that if you already live with a family containing two or three other members besides yourself then you could wait until the family are all home and start enjoying this time together. At this point it is best not to tell the rest of the group what the card and your question for guidance are all about because this would make them think about their shoes or whatever the subject was and would alter the way they acted, thereby changing the result. Sit with your chosen Dream card or cards facing your chest and tucked up the top of what you are wearing. Again using the example of the shoes you should think of the contents on the card/cards then watch the other people in the room and see what they do with their shoes? i.e. have they taken them off? Has anyone left one off and one on? Are they all wearing their shoes/slippers on their feet? If they have taken them off where have they put them? All these questions and more could be what the group of people that you are with are doing with their shoes.

If you then write these answers down on a fresh page in your notepad and compare them with your dream results, you will start to notice coincidences". As you know I believe there is no such thing as coincidence but it is in fact God or the Spirit World trying to have a quiet word with you. Hence this should sort out the answer to the question that you asked Spirit to give you the Guidance for in your dreams. One last thing that I am going to ask you to do before finishing this exercise, if it is at all possible, is to visit a place where there is a larger group of people. For example, a Spiritualist Church (although this is only one example. If you are uncomfortable with this, then a place of your choice is ok.) During the evening watch the people attending and see if you can see any reference to shoes or whatever your guidance subject is. You will be surprised how things can duplicate!! Coincidence!!? I think not!

Remember, Spirit bring their messages in what sometimes seems to be unusual ways because they make use of our brain power and logic to convey their messages. For instance, Chris and I were at a Spiritualist Church recently when after the service I was talking to the Church President and Chris decided to go to the toilet. She was gone a while then returned as I was ready to go. I said that I would pop to the toilet before we left because we had a long way to travel home. She replied: "ok, but you will have to use the other toilet which is up through the kitchen because they have just taken the door off the other one!!" I was obviously puzzled by this but said ok and we both walked out of the Mediums room together. As I went to pass the toilet that I had been to earlier I noticed that the door to the toilet where I had been to before the service, was not only on its hinges but fully intact. I noticed a confused expression on Chris's face as I said: "Look I can use this one after all." Later, I enquired what had made Chris think that the door had been taken off. She replied: "Because I went to use that toilet and the door was missing." I laughed at this but she was too confused to see the funny side at that moment in time. I asked Spirit if it was anything to do with them because this seemed the only likely explanation for something so bizarre taking place, don't you think?

Chris's Guardian Angel whom she calls Mr A immediately nodded his head in agreement, and smiling said: " She needs to learn the different ways that we can and do communicate certain information and as you know, we take the easiest route to make total use of the energies that are available to us. This was the easiest way to let her know that someone is going to get locked in this toilet and the door will have to be broken down to let them out and at the same time to let her know that the door at her home that sticks, and will end up having to be taken off to allow her to go to the bathroom if she does not get it mended. They were in fact showing her the necessity for the door to be taken off. For her to use the bathroom which would definitely be the case if it got worse because as she then informed me, her bedroom door had been sticking because the innards of the door had worked loose and kept dropping down and she sometimes struggled to get the door open to get out of the room when she needed to use the bathroom in the night. A few weeks later we attended the same Church and as I was talking to the president I asked if she would excuse me whilst I went to the toilet. She responded with: Yes but it is best to use the one round the corner because we had to break the door down on the other one when a lady from the circle got stuck in there the other night, therefore there is no longer a latch or lock on that one so you cannot close the door. Good spot of linking from Chris don't you think?

I attended a very good Spiritualist Church recently to hold a service and during that service the name Phil was called out to me whilst I was giving a lady a message from her loved ones in Spirit. She said straight away that she did not remember knowing a man called Phil. I told her that I appreciated this but this particular Phil was a lady. She however, still could not recall a Phil. At this point the lady in Spirit indicated some personal information that connected her to the lady that was with the person in the Church that day, whom I had been talking to. They sometimes do this, and as far as I am concerned that is okay provided the two people are together which they were. The other lady said that all the information that I had just given fitted in with her but she could not recall a Phil? The lady in Spirit then said I am Philomena and they called me Mini. This brought instant recognition to the lady who was receiving the message and she was so pleased to hear from her friend. If I had given up on receiving the word "no" without enquiring further, Mini's visit would have been a wasted journey whereas instead she was able to bring the happiness that she had intended with her visit.

This is the reason why when students are practising they should always remember, that in these instances, "no" does not always mean "no", it can mean that the easy route with which the Spirit visitor has chosen to come through to make the best use of the energy available, does not ring memory bells to the person here and if we work with Spirit they will bring more information through that makes it easier for them to be remembered. It is also worth mentioning here that if you are linking correctly, only Spirits who have a link no matter how tentatively to the person receiving the message are allowed to come through.

Chapter Fifteen
More Ghost Clearing

15
More Ghost Clearing

When visiting a property to send a Spirit home to the light because there have been problems of the ghost activity kind in the home or building, we have to bear three things in mind once we know for sure that there is indeed Ghost activity present, before even contemplating clearing the problem. Those three things are:

Are there one or more ghosts haunting this particular space?

Are there any frequent visits of friends or relatives in the Spirit World who are linked to the people connected to the property you are there to clear?

Has anything been left behind in the premises that belonged to the previous owners/tenants who are now in Spirit?

The reason for asking yourself these three questions is because invariably you cannot be sure that there is only one troublesome Spirit present, therefore you could send one Spirit home to the light and go home happily thinking that you have solved the problem, when in fact you have not. Secondly, sometimes it is only people who love those who are resident in the property that are causing noises etc, purely to gain attention to their presence. Last but not least it can be a problem if something that connects to the Spirit now haunting the premises is left behind even though the Spirit him or herself has gone to the light. This is because if something traumatic happened with or around the Spirit who is haunting and the object left behind connects to that Spirit and or the trauma concerned, then the vibrational pull to that Spirit will remain in the property and encourage that Spirit to re-visit the property even though they are home safe in the Spirit World and in effect no longer haunting.

On a recent visit to the home of a very nice family, I was immediately aware that, yes, there was ghost activity in the property concerned. This became increasingly obvious when whilst drinking a cup of coffee and chatting about what had been happening, suddenly the room became heavy and slightly dark in places. Everyone present felt this and we all developed a headache at the same time. Shortly afterwards, I set about clearing the house of its ghost activity. To do this, it is important to check every room in the house whilst asking questions of the occupants where necessary. Before leaving the lounge where we had been drinking our coffee I checked the room that we were in and felt that the far end of the room was not as it used to be!! It was as though it should have been a separate room. The couple who owned the house confirmed that this was definitely right because when the lady first moved in, it was indeed two separate rooms. The lounge was originally a lot smaller and there used to be a conservatory at the far end of the room, where I had felt there was a problem.

Once in the dining room, I found that again it was ok until I walked over towards the window where the vibrations were not good at all. In turn those present came over to feel, and sure enough it sent shudders rippling down everyone's spines. I was made aware that this room was also originally something different. This was confirmed with the fact that it used to be a garage. I then told them that there must have been a door that swings down to close it because a young man in Spirit made me aware of being injured when the door was pulled down on his head during a fight. Once again the owners were able to confirm that the garage door did pull downwards.

The remainder of the downstairs seemed fine so we headed towards the stair well. As I climbed onto the first stair and was about to stand on the second stair I felt a force of extreme energy push me backwards and I almost fell backwards off the stair. Some of those present also felt this once standing on the bottom stair and confirmed that a couple of members of the family had already fallen or almost fallen down these stairs. As I moved forward up the stairs I felt a discomfort that appeared to be coming from above where I was standing. As I looked up I noticed that one of the small spotlights was missing, just above my head. The gentleman of the house said that they had taken the bulb out because that particular bulb kept going out and when they replaced it, it went again and they could not see why. I smiled at this and said I think I do, but let's deal with upstairs first.

Our first stop was the master bedroom which I at first thought was ok. That is until I stood near the headboard of the bed. There, it was extremely cold and I asked if there had been any problems in that part of the room. Apparently this was where the lady of the house slept. I also asked if there had been something different there when they first moved in. She replied that there had been fitted wardrobes surrounding the headboard, which they had destroyed. I explained that there was an elderly man haunting the space because he did not know that he was dead. He used to keep his personal belongings in the wardrobe next to the bed by where his head would be. They had now pulled this down and he was feeling around with his hand searching for his stuff. She at once exclaimed that she had been lying on her back in bed one night when she woke up as someone ran the palm of their hand down the front of her face, but when she put the light on to look, there was no one there except for her husband who was fast asleep beside her and facing in the opposite direction. Although this explained the incident to her, it also made her nervous but I assured her that before I left their house that night he would have left too, and would be sent home to the light. I was then drawn to a large chest of drawers positioned at the foot of their bed. I once again felt that something different should be there too. She then explained that there were also fitted wardrobes in that part of the room.

Both of the couple's children's rooms and the bathroom had a really good feel about them and no cause for alarm. There was a little Spirit boy family member who liked to visit the Son but no problem with him. In the smallest room in the house (the toilet) there was an extreme cold feel to the back wall even though the radiator was on that wall and switched on at the time. After feeling that it was both sides of this wall that were cold, I asked Spirit about it and they said that it would be necessary to look up in the loft (I should mention that we had been hearing knocking noises coming from that direction ever since I had arrived.)

Climbing into their loft was not exceptionally difficult even for me. Once up there, I encountered the usual family treasures of old toys etc that are up in most people's lofts. At that moment all those standing around the foot of the ladder heard the knocking noises once more. I was too busy, keeping an eye on a Spirit man who had appeared from behind me, (where the knocks had been heard). He was now standing at the opposite end of the loft approximately five feet away glaring at me. I immediately summoned the help of my main Guide Mr R to help me send him home to the light because I knew that the light going out on the stairwell and the psychic energy push making people lose their balance and be in danger of falling down the stairs, was down to this man who was an angry character. He was eventually persuaded to go.

Knowing that it was now safe, I invited the others to join me up in the loft so that they could see if there was anything up in the loft area that did not belong to them. Three quarters of the loft space was very easy to see around but the space where the Spirit man had first appeared from and the bangs that could be heard, was very dark and black because the light on that side of the loft had been rendered unusable without any real explanation as to why it did not work!!! Satisfied that there was nothing remaining up there everyone descended down the ladder but as I went to follow, Mr R began to draw my attention to the dark corner of the loft once again as if there was definitely something there connected to the previous people who lived in the house. One of which was the man who was haunting the loft space for some reason as well as other parts of the house. The man of the house said "You are not sure that it is clear are you Jean?" To which I replied "No I am not. Have you by any chance got a torch that I may borrow?"

He replied that they did not have a torch, but Chris reminded me that she had a small one in her car for map reading. I told her that it would be perfect, and she at once fetched it from the car. Once I was able to shine a light into the darkness of the corner of the loft behind where the approach from up the ladder, I could clearly see a pile of wooden flooring planks. I asked if they knew what they were? Once again the family of the house joined me up the loft and I asked if the man could go across and move the planks whilst being careful. After asking why he should be careful and being told by me that this was purely so that he did not fall through the ceiling, the man gingerly made his way over to remove the wooden planks, after first asking me if Spirit were gone from there because it made him nervous, and being reassured by me that they had. He started to pass them across to his wife who passed them to her son to pass them to Chris who was still at the foot of the ladder. Then suddenly he shouted that he had found something that was definitely not theirs underneath the pile of wooden boards. He had found a huge piece of carpet. They all looked at it and declared that it did not belong to them so I told them that it had to go. As soon as it was removed the whole atmosphere cleared to a light and care free one up in their loft. Once down stairs again the lady realised that she recognised the carpet as being the same carpet that had originally been in the conservatory where all the bad feelings downstairs had been emanating from. Problem solved, and now this wonderful family could get on with their lives without Spirit intrusion.

It was Tuesday evening on 5th July 2005 and my close friend Sue was picking me up to take me to her Sister Jo's house because she had recently moved into her new home and was having problems with what appeared to be ghost activity. Upon our arrival at Jo's new home, we started off by doing what any sensible human being would do. We stopped for a coffee prepared lovingly by the girl's mum Grace, so that we could chat about things that had taken place since their arrival to Jo's new home. Whilst partaking of our drink Jo explained that at first she felt really safe and comfortable in her recently acquired residence, then one day she was sitting on the toilet which is situated on the first floor facing the stairwell to the upper level. Because she was 'home alone, or so she thought!!!' she had left the door open and was happily aware of the sun and the warmth that it brought with it, which was shining from the windows from the landing which is halfway up to the next level. When suddenly it went icy cold, yet as she quickly looked up to the window she could see that the sun was still shining. She shuddered from the inside out and hurried to go back to the kitchen and normality!!!

Grace was helping Jo to decorate her newly acquired home and the next day she returned to the lounge where she had been painting after paying a visit to the toilet. There in front of her eyes where the paint pot was standing she saw the paintbrush move yet it was in a position where it could not fall or slide over, and we also have to bear in mind that she had been out of the room for several minutes, therefore if it was going to move it would have already done so!! The position that it was now in was not how it had been when she left the room. Both women had the distinct feeling from then on that someone was following them around Jo's new home, wherever they went and Jo's young son became afraid to sleep in his bedroom in their new home. It was at this point that Jo was shocked by a thundering crash coming from what sounded like upstairs. She phoned her mum and got her to talk to her whilst she checked upstairs. However, nothing untoward was found but they decided that it was time to ask me to come and check it out for them, and do what we jokingly refer to as 'a bit of ghost busting.'

Coffee and talk over, and now it was time for action. On checking, it was discovered that there was a lot of aggressive energy in the area in one of the bedroom's wall and near to the wardrobe. I was made aware of a young boy in Spirit who was drawing my attention to a door that in my opinion was in an unusual place. This being so because the bottom of the door was at least three foot away from the floor. It appeared to be in mid air and it would be quite difficult to reach into because of this fact. The boy made it clear that he had frequently been locked inside this wardrobe when it was considered that he was misbehaving, but I suspect by the way that this information came across, that he was not really naughty at all, just in the way. Unfortunately he met an untimely death due to his harsh treatment after suffering with pneumonia. It was at that time extremely cold in that cupboard where he was left to spend many hours with little or nothing to do or eat. When Jo and her two beautiful sons moved into their new home, the Spirit of this boy became excited by the fact that these boys and their Mother who was obviously kinder than his own Mother ever was, would perhaps treat him kindly. It is unfortunate but it frequently happens that when trying to be noticed, a Spirit like this young boy, often make a lot of noise and or create a strange cold atmosphere to manifest whenever they are actively around. Then instead of just enjoying their new companionship they end up scaring their new friends. Remember that when young children see Spirit visitors and talk to them people have a tendency to suggest that they are talking to an imaginary friend. This is much easier and less scary to most people than having to admit that maybe they have ghost activity where they live, and this is where the child's invisible friend is really from. To that ghost who is only a Spirit haunting the space where they come from, because they do not realise that they are in fact dead, it is hard to understand why new people are now in their space. They then look on people here almost like their own imaginary friends who are invading their space. The reversal of roles factor can often come into play where Spirit visitors are concerned when people here are moving into and/or residing in what they think and feel is their space.

Ring any bells!!!? Maybe, just maybe we are their imaginary friends and not the other way round. After all, who is to say that they are in our space and not the other way round? Did the chicken come before the egg or vice versa? Do we come before Spirit or vice versa? Are they our imaginary friends, or are we theirs? Interesting theory don't you think? I gently encouraged the boy to go home to the light and was really pleased when I became aware that his Grandmother in the Spirit World came to meet him and take care of him in the Spirit World, which is a delightfully happy ending to a life and subsequent death of misery for that lovely little boy.

After checking the whole of Jo's new home it became blatantly obvious that it would be necessary for me to investigate what was happening in the loft area. Unfortunately at that time it was extremely difficult for me to climb up into lofts, so Sue bravely went up and I climbed far enough up the ladder so that my head and shoulders were inside the loft area and I could see and be in control of anything that took place. There was a lot of rubbish that had been left up the loft by the previous owners/tenants which would make the job at hand more difficult but Sue bravely agreed to carry on. At first she was stooping down warily, looking around her to see what she could see. It was very dark up there and although we had a torch there was not really enough light for us to take care of the job in hand. So I called down to Jo and Grace who were eagerly waiting at the foot of the ladder in case we needed assistance. They looked around and eventually handed me a table lamp minus its shade so that we could use it like an extra torch. This was much better and seemed to do the trick.

First of all I asked Sue to check behind me for any sign of anything that should not be there because I was aware that Mr R was a little uncertain about my awareness of the situation. Then as she was going through the debris around the loft there were certain things that needed to be extricated so we passed them down to Jo and Grace so that they could take them out for disposal. At one point Sue who was becoming braver as time went on, was walking across the loft in a semi stoop when my Silver backed gorilla called Abundwi, who is my Spirit protection animal started to growl from behind me. His growl was so loud and prominent that even Sue heard him and although she knows of his existence, she had never actually heard him before. She immediately ducked back down and said "Did you hear that growl then, Jean?" I assured her that yes I had heard it but it was only Abundwi warning us to be careful. Spirit made me aware of the back wall of the loft saying that it needed investigating. I asked Sue if she would prefer me to try and get up to check but she bravely said no she would manage because she knew that this would be difficult for me. I guess that is a sign of a true friend to risk danger rather than place me in harm's way. She tentatively made her way across towards the wall to find that there was a board leaning up against it blocking off a hole that led to the loft next door. I suggested that it was a good idea to feel inside just in case anything had been placed there. Sue's look said it all. I told her that if she did not want to risk putting her hand inside, then she should find something to poke inside the hole with, and true to form she looked around and gently picked up a piece of gas pipe that was nearby and carefully poked inside the hole. She assured me that the hole was clear and I told her to block the entrance up with rags and paper that were around her. She did this before placing the board back against the wall to hide the now blocked hole from view.

This done she turned to head back towards the trapdoor and me, when all of a sudden, Abundwi growled and beat his chest which was quite audible even to Sue who had once again dived down into a crouching position, her hair had become more curly than her usual beautiful curly locks. Then as if by magic, the whole of one side of the loft lit up as if a light had been switched on and a pile of clothes was visible in the far corner, and we clearly heard the name Sam called in a scary voice. All went dark again and I stretched up further into the loft trapdoor trying to light up that same corner with my lamp torch as Sue slowly went over to investigate. Once there she found some old clothes which she carried over to me to pass out of the loft for disposal. She said that she had finished apart from an old Bible which was underneath the clothes. I asked her to bring it over to me, so that we could look at it in the light.

As I turned the pages I came across some pages that had been scribbled on and said to Sue, "look at this", and we both went cold as we realised that the pages which had been scribbled on were those containing the story of Sam and Saul. The part of the page of the Bible that was scribbled on was 1 Samuel, chapter 9-25/26 where Samuel called Saul to the top of the house where they communed and he told him 'up, that I may send thee away.' Remember that we had heard the name Sam called out just before we discovered the old Bible, and we were in the loft which is at the top of the house, and communicating with the Spirits to send them away. Sue was an amazing help that day but I swear she came down from that loft with her hair even curlier than she went up!

One day in January I was called out to clear a disturbance that the family believed was being created by ghost activity in 'what was' a fairly new home to the people who lived in the house in Birmingham. When the evening arrived for the appointment, I set off for the house feeling a little excited because of the nature of the information I had received regarding the ghost or ghosts who were causing the problem for the new owners of the house. I never go to the homes of people whom I do not know alone because in this day and age you cannot be too careful and as I have explained in my previous books, I learned this the hard way through a few bad experiences. This was, I am afraid, with the living and not the dead. On this occasion, Chris, (my very good friend and PA came along to support and as she was developing her Spiritual gifts I came to the conclusion that it would double up as good experience for her.

On the day that the gentleman had been given my card as a possible person to help with their problem, he took his wife a bunch of flowers home which she was delighted with and placed them in a vase, leaving them standing on the kitchen counter so that they could go out for a family meal and deal with the flowers properly later. George also explained to Jane that he had spoken to a gentleman who had told him that I would exorcise his ghost if anyone could. He had been given my card, as I said earlier, and he handed it to his wife who immediately placed it on the kitchen counter next to the flowers, ready for them to contact me on their return. However, when the family arrived home after their meal out, they were welcomed by the fact that the flowers were on the kitchen floor and my card was nowhere to be found. That is until they went to the bin to dispose of the debris left by the scattered flowers, and lo and behold, there was my card. Even this young couple who did not have a lot of experience to do with the Spirit World, and before this had been sceptical to say the least, knew that Spirit were telling them not to contact me. However, after speaking to the person who had given them the card they asked him if he would contact me which he duly did.

As soon as we entered the house that Thursday evening I was aware of an icy coldness which is often found where ghost activity resides. The couple asked if we would like a cup of tea or coffee which we accepted. As I have said before where possible I always sit and chat to the home occupiers for a while before doing anything else, therefore a cup of coffee is always welcome. The reason for this chat is so that I can find out exactly what has been happening in their home according to their opinion. They do after all live in the property and know what strange things are taking place if any? We have to remember that what seems to be obviously ghost activity to the layman is not always a fact once I investigate. There are for instance occasions when the person who has contacted me is suffering from mental health problems and does not have a ghost present in their home at all. On these occasions I have to tactfully suggest that the person needs to visit their doctor. I have to say though that thankfully the amount of times that this has been necessary I can count on one hand. At other times it can be something as simple as the central heating rattling or the wind blowing through a gap in the roof or windows of the home with the problem. Or even noises coming from the flat above, below or next door, to the supposed haunted property. So you see talking to the person or people can be a great help. Secondly, if I chat to the people for a while it helps to make them feel at home and settle any fears they may have about my presence and attempt at clearing their ghostly apparition.

On this particular occasion, as we sat opposite a fire that was giving out considerable heat which both Chris and I could feel, I was aware of an icy cold draught which I knew could not be accounted for by the fact that my Guide Mr R was standing extremely close because it was a different type of cold. It was a chill where you could feel a lot of tension, and hostility aimed towards you being there. This would never be the case with Mr R, even on the occasions when he becomes irritated with me. I asked Chris and the couple if they could feel it and they all confirmed that they could. We listened with interest as they relayed their stories of the incidents which had and were still taking place in the home which was to be their dream home when they purchased it eight months earlier. After listening and talking to the couple whilst drinking our welcome beverages I asked if it was possible for me to visit the bathroom before we got started. They of course agreed and as I headed towards the stairs I noticed that Chris was smiling to herself. I was later to learn that this smile was because she knew me well enough to know that if I want to talk in peace with the Spirit world I do so in the bathroom because I learned a long time ago that Spirit work well close to water and they always talk to me there. On this occasion she was right although I also needed to use the toilet.

As I sat on the toilet in the hopes of a quiet chat with Mr R and company I was surprised to feel a large surge of cold go across my lower back. Once again I knew that this Spirit was a stranger to me and not my Guides and helpers. I now knew beyond a shadow of a doubt that there was hostile ghost activity in this house. I headed down stairs and without saying anything about my experience in their sparkling new bathroom at that point, I suggested that we all go upstairs so that my investigations into their problems could begin. Jane made me smile because she immediately asked if I wanted her to put all the lights out because she had seen something similar to this on the television. I replied that we did not need the lights off, in fact I preferred them on, so that I could see what I was doing. I have the ability to see Spirit in a room with a light on because I see them objectively which means solidly like a person who is still alive. If however, I had been attempting to sensationalise what I was doing it would be better with the lights off because the dark allows people to mobilise the infra-red part of their eyes more, allowing them to see or think they see something which they may not recognise when the lights are on. I was not there to frighten these people any more than they were already, just to sort out their problems making their home liveable for them and send any Spirit or Spirits home towards the light where they can find peace. However, I must indicate here that there are times when darkness is necessary because the ghost in question only visits when it is dark, therefore switching off the lights will encourage them to come forward.

Our first port of call when we arrived upstairs was the occupiers two sons bedroom where George had reported noticing a strange smell even though the whole house including that bedroom had been totally gutted and re-plastered. The first thing that was very noticeable when we entered the room was a very large fitted wardrobe all along one wall that had ceiling to floor mirrors for doors across its full length. This is a mistake in a room that is haunted because it allows the visiting Spirits to cast shadows to try to get your attention. Mostly people think that they have imagined these shadows but it does not stop Spirit from trying to catch your eye. As I stood in the doorway with my three interested followers (Chris, Jane, and George) close behind, I noticed a presence in the corner of the room near to the window. In order not to frighten my team of eager followers I did not say that there was a Spirit in the room other than the Guides that were accompanying us. Instead I walked over to the corner where I could see the visitor. There was a window across the back wall and a gap about twelve inches long on the adjacent wall between the window and the start of the large wardrobes that I mentioned earlier. As I moved forward I could smell the aroma that George had reported noticing in the room. Sure enough it was the pungent albeit gentle smell that is often associated with Spirit presence when they have resided in the area for a long time.

First of all I asked Chris to come forward to see if she could smell anything which she could not, the couple came forward one at a time. George could smell it slightly but Jane, like Chris, could not. As I returned to the corner to investigate I was aware of a young man in the Spirit World who had the back of his head caved in. He indicated that he had fallen from a great height through glass and no one seemed to care. I immediately tried to explain to him that he had died in the fall and was in fact dead so therefore not visible to most living people, therefore it was not that they did not care but because they could not see him. As he stepped forward the pain through my head to my eye was tremendous and I asked him to step back, which with reluctance he did, before disappearing and reappearing several times through the bedroom ceiling.

After telling the young couple about their Spirit lodger they told me that it sounded like the son of the previous owners. He had in fact fallen to his death through a roof and through glass. I asked George if there was anything up the loft because the Spirit was still floating up and down through the ceiling and I felt that it was not purely because he had fallen to his death through a roof but that he had spent a lot of time up the loft for some reason. He said that there was nothing at all up the loft because they had checked. At that point I cleared the atmosphere in the room stating that I would return to that room later then asked if we could check the bathroom next.

On entering the bathroom I returned to stand near to the toilet where I had felt the icy draught before and sure enough it was there as strong as ever. I asked Chris over first and she agreed that it was a very strong sensation that would be difficult to miss. The couple agreed. The window was up that end of the room but it was a high window which meant that the draught could not have been coming from that window especially when you consider that if we moved our hands up the wall towards the window ledge we could no longer feel it. At that point I saw quite clearly a picture of a man slightly bent over struggling to get into the bath along the wall where the sink and toilet were and not the bath.

I explained this to the owners of the house and they said that the bath was under the window when they moved into the house eight months earlier but they had taken it out and put a new one in along the other wall to make more space. I then told them that the man was slightly shorter than George but it was difficult to tell for sure because he was bent over a little after having what I thought was a stroke. I also reported that he was generally a gentle quiet man but he had become aggressive and angry after the illness took away his ability to look after himself, making it necessary for him to rely on his wife for his basic care needs. Once again they could confirm this because the husband of the previous owner had suffered a stroke changing him totally and he had finally died in the house. He did not want to go to the light because he was waiting for his wife to come home. This was because he was not aware that he had died and his wife had in fact moved out. Eventually, however, with the help of Mr R he went home to the light. At that point I saw the young man going up and down to the loft once more, so repeated twice that I needed them to be sure that there was nothing up their loft. They assured me on both occasions that there was not.

Our next room for investigation was the main bedroom which was ok until I was over by the window when at first I was aware of a young girl whom I felt was associated with the family who owned the house before the previous owners. There was also a young Irish man whom I felt belonged to the same family. I was told that this family were definitely Irish. I asked if there had been some aggression with the lady of the family towards the next door neighbour. Jane said that she did not know but she would later ask the neighbours who were still living next door. Finally I asked if the man who had fallen through the roof had a brother who was unwell because I was aware of them by the front bedroom window. Jane said that yes he did have a brother who had been involved in an accident and the two brothers shared the front bedroom. I sent the little girl quite easily to the light but the Irish man who had been killed during a fight was quite aggressive in his attitude towards me so once again I called for the help of Mr R, who succeeded very quickly in sending him home to the light. We checked the small bedroom next which was quite tiny, and apart from Jane's Nan stopping for a chat, I was relieved to find that this room was clear of any ghost activity. However as I was walking back out onto the landing the young man was once again going up and down through the ceiling into the loft. Once again I enquired if they were sure that there was nothing in the loft because sometimes it is things being left behind up the loft that cause the problem and I felt reasonably sure that this was the case in this instance.

George fetched the ladders so that I could see for myself so that I would be satisfied that the loft was clear whilst I was there. There was not much space to get up the loft because it was close to the banister so Chris said that she would stick her head up as she thought that it would be too dangerous for me with my health issues. I asked if she was sure because I know that she is terrified of heights but she insisted and the three of us held her legs secure whilst she tensely climbed the ladder slowly a rung at a time. Once her head was through what was a very small hatch she decided that she would need to climb up yet one more rung because the roof lagging was so thick that she could not see over it. She steadily pulled herself up one more rung with torch in hand ready to search the dark and eerie loft for any item or items that may have been left behind that could be causing the Spirit of the young man to become anxious about.

Chris immediately declared that she could see what looked like a big grey plastic box at the far end of the loft. At this George said to Chris that if she came down he would climb up and take a look. It turned out that there was a camping gas cooker approximately twelve inches long, six inches wide and three inches deep with a steel funnel lying next to it about one foot long and four inches circular up the loft. There was also a large bottle gas heater and some boards had been placed up in the loft to sit on. As I had suggested earlier, the young man had spent a lot of time up in the loft using the heater to keep warm and the camping gas cooker to make a drink when he wanted one. The problem was that these items are dangerous things to leave up a loft in case the heat of the sun catches them alight and burns the house down. It is also very dangerous to have highly combustible items around when there is a high level of ghost activity in the area as there was here.

George passed the camping gas cooker down to me followed by the funnel. Then I excused myself and went to the bathroom. A couple of minutes later as I was drying my hands I heard a tremendous bang and a yell from Chris. I raced out onto the landing to see Chris standing nursing a cut with blood pouring everywhere. What had happened was George passed the gas bottle heater down to Chris in its black bag, which was no problem whatsoever. But as Chris went to bring it down to the ground there was a sudden force against the side of the bag and the side of the heater which was made of sheet metal shot sideways over the banister and down the stairs catching Chris' finger as it did so. Fortunately there was no-one down at the bottom of the stairwell otherwise there could have been a very serious and nasty accident.

Spirit were getting very anxious about what we were doing and when this happens they give off a lot more psychic energy which is like static electricity. This rebounds towards us and reacts against our Aura which is magnetic. In this case this happening caused the front of the heater to be hurled down the stairs. It must be remembered that it is the energy that throws the item or items and not the Spirit World becoming violent. Apart from two pieces of paper with a 1979 date on them the loft was now clear and I asked them to make sure that the items were disposed of away from the house.

Once George had returned from the loft onto the landing, I told them that it was time to go back into the room where the smell was. As I walked towards the corner the smell hit me much stronger than before so I asked Chris to come over once again. This time she declared with a certain amount of pleasure that YES she could smell the aroma. Jane could also smell it and neither of these ladies could detect anything when we were in the room previously. It was now time to work on sending the visitor home to the light with the help of Mr R.

At this point the lady and man who had lived next door for many years came up to talk to me. I described the man who had the stroke and she agreed that he was the husband of the last owner. As I spoke to her about the previous owners she said that yes she had had problems with the Irish lady who had lived there. She told me that I was right when I said that the lady was upset with her and aggressive. She told me that she was upset with her for tying a break in the fence with a bit of string until she could get it repaired. The Irish lady got so upset that the police had to be called to sort the problem out. At that moment I saw BETTY written above the neighbour's head and she told me that yes this was the Irish previous owner but one's, name.

As we headed downstairs Jane asked if I could check the lounge one more time and I agreed. However, as I came to the bottom of the stairs Mr R reminded me that I had not been in the Kitchen, so I asked George if this was ok and he responded with 'Of course you can Jean this has always been the coldest room in the house even with the central heating and the oven on.' I walked into what was an L shaped room and the second half contained the sink, oven, and kitchen appliances. He was right, it was icy cold in there and Chris agreed. As I stepped towards the sink I felt a sharp pain shoot from my ear to my neck and stepped backwards. I asked Chris to stand where I had been and she too got the sharp pain from her ear to her neck. I then saw a large old fashioned square sink in the place where the small modern round sink now was. George confirmed that there was a sink of that description there when they moved in. I then felt that the kitchen was not where I was standing. Once again he confirmed that the original kitchen was up the first part of the kitchen where there was now a dining room. I was made aware that the young man used to clean his engine parts in the old square sink. He therefore was haunting this space, and his Mum's bedroom and the loft most of all. The kitchen and loft because he spent a lot of time there and his Mum's bedroom because he was looking for her.

You will remember if you have read my previous books that mostly Ghosts do not haunt people they haunt spaces. This is because they generally do not realise that they are dead and cannot find their way home to the light. This is where Mediumistic people like me are called in to send them home to the light and put them to rest. Interestingly enough only two nights earlier Chris had dreamed that she was moving house and that in the dream someone whom you would least expect to give their money away, insisted that they gave her £30 to help with her travelling expenses. After I cleared the ghosts in the house above, the owners insisted on giving me some money to help with the travelling expenses and lo and behold they gave me £30. Another coincidence maybe, but I do not think so, do you?

I received a telephone call from a Spiritualist Church President who explained to me that a gentleman came to see him at the Church because he was having trouble with ghost activity in his home. Apparently the family had called in the local priest twice, only to find that if anything things seemed to get worse as far as their ghostly apparitions were concerned. When called to visit the house for the third time, the priest refused because he said he was afraid of the goings-on in the house

Another religious group also declined their offer to visit the house with the intention of clearing these particular ghosts. So the President of the Spiritualist Church told the man that he would telephone me to enquire as to whether I could help in this instance, because he knew that I had been able to help in other similar incidences. I of course agreed to help and arranged to visit the home of this family with my team. As I have said before, upon first arriving at any place where I am asked to help with ghost activity of any kind, my first request is that we sit with a cup of coffee and discuss what has been happening in the place where the haunting is said to be. I have already given my reasons for this. However, on this occasion, firstly I needed to let the people involved get used to me and my team and know what is going to be happening. You would be surprised at how many strange ideas go around about what happens when someone like myself, comes to clear ghost activity. For instance many people expect me to bring lots of equipment with me, when in reality this is not necessary. Secondly so that I would get the opportunity to link into my Guides and to any Spirits that may be around at that time, in the place where I am visiting, before I start work with those Spirit visitors.

During this chat over a cup of coffee I ask questions that are pertinent to the reason why I am there. For instance one of the questions that I usually ask is: if a family have been living in their home for a long time but have only recently started to experience a lot of ghost activity there, has anyone who lives in the house been using a Ouija board? This is important because it is sometimes an immediate answer as to why the ghosts are suddenly making their presence known to the household members. I also enquire what ages any children or young adults in the house are, because young people can produce a lot of psychic energy which gives Spirits the opportunity to let the living know that they are there when it has not been possible before. Thirdly I ask if there has been any conflict in the home recently because again this produces a lot of psychic energy for the Spirits to work with. Last but not least I ask what problems the resident people have been experiencing.

Unfortunately many people decide to play with Ouija boards without knowing what they are doing. They tend to look on it as some sort of game, when it is not. When using a Ouija board without a qualified Medium being present you are literally calling up any Spirit that wishes to come whether they are good or bad. This quite often leads to problems because once the Spirit has answered the person using the board's request to visit and the person here does not know how to send them away again which a qualified Medium would be able to do, this then unfortunately frequently causes the person to be haunted by the person they have invited. Hence Spirit Activity that was not noticed previously suddenly occurs. It should be pointed out that generally ghosts haunt spaces not people but in the case of a Spirit being called up by a Ouija board they actually haunt the person or people who used the Ouija board to call them up.

As far as young people being present is concerned, this is quite simply because young people create a lot of psychic energy due to changing hormones etc. This is because psychic energy is like static electricity which tends to rebound off the youngsters Aura because our Aura is a magnetic energy field around us. If a Spirit comes close within our Auric field the static electricity effect rebounds off the magnets within our Aura and this alters our metabolism. If a young person is excitable because of their hormone changes this effect can act in reverse. In other words the magnets in the Aura are producing a lot of energy which attracts the psychic energy or static electricity towards it which in turn gives the Spirit or Spirits energy to manifest themselves so that they can now be heard, seen, or sensed by the people in the building where they are haunting. It follows the same pattern as with young people if there is conflict occurring. For instance, if a couple are arguing more than usual this can produce the energy that is needed for the above to happen.

Once I have been given some idea as to what I am dealing with, I can safely get on with the job in hand. It is now time to look around the part of the building that is being haunted. In the case of this house it was the upstairs. There were two bedrooms and a bathroom upstairs and a trap door leading to the loft. As I walk around I am feeling for any energies good or bad that are present and linking to see whether I am aware of any Spirit activity at that time. In this particular home a young three year old boy said that the devil was up the loft and the couple of the house had been aware of shadows in the bedroom and the fact that the bedroom frequently went darker during the night as these two shadows appeared next to the woman's side of the bed.

Her husband had even moved the bed around to another part of the room to help her feel at ease but this did not help because the two shadows one of which was tall and one short still came and stood next to the lady's side of the bed and the room still went dark on these occasions. I was already aware that it could be possible for there to be problems because of the nature of the troubles that the family were having and because the man of the family and his friends had been using a Ouija board in the house some four years earlier and things had started to build up from that time onwards. Therefore anyone at all could have been called up.

There was a slight energy on the landing and on the wall of the second bedroom that backed onto the main bedroom where the shadows had been showing themselves. The bathroom seemed clear and in the main bedroom there were definite energies that showed Spirit activity was present. I asked the man to take the cover off the loft entrance which he did and also switched on the light up there. Usually by this point I am very aware of problems up the loft if there are any. There did not appear to be any problems even though the little boy had seen someone up the loft. The owner of the house did not have a ladder for us to go up into the loft and as there did not seem to be any problems up there anyway I decided not to worry about it and deal with the main bedroom where the problem seemed to be.

As I have already stated, most of the time when clearing ghost activity, contrary to belief, it does not need to be dark. Any good Medium can detect a Spirit and send them home to the light with all the synthetic lights on. On this occasion however the Spirits seemed to be standing back and because they mainly showed themselves at night. I decided that we should imitate the conditions that they appeared to use, ie: when it is dark. The couple whose bedroom it was, usually slept with the door slightly ajar, so that there was a slight beam of light coming through into the room from a light that was left on in the downstairs hallway. Therefore, we simulated these conditions which left the bedroom semi dark. To start off with the man whose bedroom it was stayed in the room. There was also my team, which on that occasion were Chris and Richard who was a camera man and of course myself. I was just inside the room with Chris to my left and Richard to my right. The man whom the bedroom belonged to was standing about a foot away from the bottom of the bed, he was between the window and the bottom of the bed.

Straight away a lady came through and although she was upset and did visit regularly she was not the one who was causing the worrying ghost activity. She was in fact the sister of the man whose bedroom it was. As we talked to his sister the man started to feel nauseous which, happens a lot when Spirits are haunting. At this point I could see a Spirit man and hear a boy and told the man who was feeling really ill by this point and had to sit down on the end of the bed. I decided that it was wiser if he went downstairs and after checking that he was ok sent him down. He is a very psychic man and was therefore picking up these senses very strongly.

At this point his wife joined us in the room and we moved to the area at the bottom of the bed so that she could stand where we had been standing. Almost straight away the tall man appeared in the room and laid claim to being the tall shadow that stood next to the lady's bed at night. He told me that he was her brother and had died suddenly in his forties and came regularly to visit her. With the other information that he was able to give, the lady who frequently saw the shadows agreed that it was her brother. At that point a boy appeared and approached where I was standing and as he did so the room went dark. Richard called out "Jean it has gone dark!" This made me smile because it was Richard's first time at anything like this because he had replaced the usual cameraman at short notice.

As we travelled to the house he had said that he was not sure that he believed in the existence of Spirit yet here he was telling me that the room had gone dark as soon as I said that the young Spirit boy had entered the room. As Richard spoke the boy backed off and the room went back to how it was before.

The boy was nine years of age and had been hung in a tree with a cord around his neck, by some bullies and left there where he consequently hung to death. He had been missing for a few hours before his body was found hanging from the tree. When I told the lady his name and everything about him she told me that he was her cousin who had in fact been killed in that way. She told me that one of the lads who hung him in the tree about nine years earlier had in fact grown up and committed suicide because he could not cope with what he had done to the young boy.

It is unusual for people haunting after being called up on Ouija boards to belong to the people they are haunting but the young lad had not arrived home in the Spirit world properly and was lost so was attracted by the Ouija board and found his way to his Aunt. This is why it was the lady's side of the bed where the shadows appeared. It was her nephew and it was her brother who was taking care of this young man now he was dead. The reason the three year old boy thought that it was the devil was purely because the boy in Spirit was playing games with him and the child thought that it was for real. The family tell me that their home is now quiet and safe again after our visit. This is because the little boy and the man were both lost and have now been sent home safely to the light where they are happy and at peace. Although needless to say these Spirit relatives still visit their family on occasions.

Whilst in the USA on a recent visit, I was asked if it would be possible for me to go and take a look at a lady's home that appeared to be haunted. She had been aware of a dark shadow walking into the bedroom and standing looking at her from the doorway. I of course said yes and arranged to go to see her after Demonstrating in the local Spiritualist Church. The lady in question had a beautiful home and the kitchen and lounge had a really good feel about it. This was obviously a good start because it meant that if indeed the house was haunted it would only be part of the home and not the whole property. The reason that this is good is quite simply because they are usually easier to send home to the light when confined to one area of the property instead of everywhere. After my obligatory cup of coffee and chat we headed off to look around. In the office I was first greeted by the Spirit of the lady of the house's partner who was now in Spirit. He however, was not haunting, but merely visiting and watching over the lady he loves and has left behind. After conversing with the lady about the gentleman whom she was very pleased to hear from, we moved on to another part of the house. Whilst passing through the hallway I was aware of a bad vibration but decided to come back to it later, and went on to one of the bedrooms which was being used to perform massages (because the lady whose home it was is a masseur,) and not as a bedroom. At first I was aware of a lady who once lived in a house built on the land of the property I was now in. Although she needed sending home to the light I was not too worried about her presence, and did just that; sent her home to the light. Bedroom two was ok and Ghost free without any help from me, which was good. We then headed back through the hall way where once again I was aware of the bad feeling and into the master bedroom of the property, which was the bedroom slept in by the lady of the house.

Although just inside of the bedroom close to the hallway did not feel too good, the rest of the room and en-suite felt good. I came back over to the side of the bedroom where the problem seemed to be. I should explain that it is rare for me not to see the actual Spirit causing the problem. However, this time I could not see anyone but could feel this really bad presence. Along the bedroom wall just inside the door was a fitted walk-in wardrobe with a door near to the bedroom door. I asked the lady if any changes had been made to that side of the room. She at once said 'no.' I told her that I did not understand this because Mr R was making me aware of the change to the room and not just furniture being changed round but a constructional change. At that point she got excited and said that there used to be two doors to the walk-in wardrobe when she first moved in but she had had one taken out and plastered up because she did not feel that two were needed.

I now knew that the problem was in the wardrobe just the other side of the hall wall. I told her this and asked if I could look inside, which she agreed to. Once inside I looked around and asked if anything in that wardrobe had been left in the property by the previous owners. At first she answered 'no' but when I said I felt that there would be a place where a weapon could be hidden, she replied yes under all this pile of blankets there is a safe that for some reason the previous owners left behind. I was now being told that the previous lady of the house was very depressed after the loss of a loved one and had attempted suicide with a gun that was kept in the safe. This had left an impression and whenever her loved ones in Spirit visited it created energy for Spirit to show themselves. They were in fact trying to protect and look after the new owner of the house. She immediately retorted that she would throw the safe out, and I explained to her that this was not necessary. All she would have to do was mix together a solution of vinegar and water, then wash the safe all over, inside and out with the liquid, then wash it off with clear water. This would in fact do the job of clearing the vibration and in turn would make the loved ones of the previous owners realise that she is no longer there or in danger from anything inside the safe; allowing them to find and visit and protect her where she now lives.

I feel that it is necessary to point out here that just because you see a dark shadow moving through your home, or indeed standing watching you, it does not necessarily mean that you have a bad Spirit in your home. The lady had seen the shadow by her bedroom door whilst she was in bed settling down to sleep.

I have explained before that whilst asleep we are on the same vibration where the Spirit World reside. This means that once we start to get sleepy we become aware of Spirit's vibration. Whilst in this sleepy state, we are in-between being awake and asleep so therefore are caught momentarily between two worlds. Because of this fact we are neither fully on one vibration or the other, so therefore when we see Spirit we cannot possibly see them objectively (solidly) because we are not fully on the vibration where they reside. This means that we see them subjectively (opaquely) instead. By this I mean that we see their outline, and the vibrational shift that is them. This in turn makes it appear to be a black shadow. So you see the lady was not being haunted by a dark entity, even though there was a bad feeling near to where the ghost always appeared. She is indeed a very lucky lady because she has a great ability which allows her to see our Spirit visitors and can train this ability should she so wish.

Chapter Sixteen
Back To Work

16
Back to Work

For this exercise you are going to need your cards and your writing pad, plus twenty six envelopes, (the size should be big enough to hold one of your Jean Kelford Dream cards).

1) Write from number one to twenty six on the twenty six Envelopes so that it can be seen clearly.

2) Take cards one to twenty six out of your pack and put them to one side. This will leave you the remaining eighteen cards in your second pile.

3) Using the first twenty six cards take out the cards that coincide with your two initials or the two initials of the person whom you are trying to read for and place them to one side. You should now have three separate stacks of cards. one with twenty four cards, one with eighteen cards and one with two cards.

In other words my initials are JK so therefore I would take out card 10 and 11, because J is the tenth letter in the alphabet and K is the eleventh letter in the alphabet. The cards that coincide with your initials give information as to what you should be doing to follow your life's pathway at that present time when you are reading your cards. As already shown earlier these are what my two cards say:

Card 10:
DREAM VIBRATIONS

Your dream vibrations are bringing a loved one in Spirit close to you right now.

Think of the person whom you most want to hear from in the Spirit World before you go to sleep for three consecutive nights. That person will appear in your dreams and Guide you forward in life.

Card 11:
EXPECT THE BEST

You will receive what you expect to receive right now so expect the best.

The energies around you at this moment are exceptionally good but you will only get what you expect, so make the effort to expect the best and the effort will be made for the best to occur.

When put together they say:

Your dream vibrations are bringing a loved one in Spirit close to you right now. You will receive what you expect to receive so expect the best.

And the more in depth version is:

Think of the person whom you most want to hear from in the Spirit World before you go to sleep for three consecutive nights. That person will appear in your dreams and Guide you forward in life. The energies around you at this moment are exceptionally good but you will only get what you expect, so make the effort to expect the best and the effort will be made for the best to occur.

Once again I am being reminded about Spirit being able to Guide me, and I am being told to look out for the good things to happen because I will get what I expect. This is the part of my pathway that I should be taking notice of. However, at this point you should ignore that information, because we are trying to analyse what we are receiving for ourselves or others apart from this and not taking notice of this particular part of our pathway.

4)   Shuffle the pile with eighteen cards in, and fan them out face down in front of you.

5)   Choose two of the fanned out cards at random that you are drawn to.

6)   Add the two cards that you have chosen to your pile of twenty four cards, now making a stack of twenty six cards again. You should now have sixteen cards in the remaining pack

7)   Shuffle your twenty six envelopes, whilst trying not to look at the numbers on them.

8)   Now shuffle your pile of twenty six cards again, without looking at which cards they are.

9)   Place one card in each envelope by taking the card off the top of the stack of twenty six cards and the envelope off the top of your pile of envelopes, and marrying them together until all twenty six are done, without looking at the cards.

10) Shuffle the remaining sixteen cards and fan them face down in front of you.

11) Now is the time for you to close your eyes for a moment or two, and think about the question or problem that you would like Guidance with.

12) Opening your eyes, manoeuvre your hand palm down approximately one inch above your fan of sixteen cards. Going slowly backward, and forwards until you feel the desire to stop and take out a card. Place the card face down in front of you separately

from the fanned out cards. Repeat number twelve a second time. Place your second card face down to the right of your first card, leaving enough space for two more cards to go in between.

14) Take up your envelopes and shuffle them whilst your eyes are closed, taking out two envelopes one at a time whenever you feel the desire to do so.

15) Take the card out of the first envelope that you chose and place it face down to the right of your first card, then take the second card out and place it to the right of that one. (This means that these two cards are in between your previous two cards and you now have four cards in a row.)

16) Now take the two cards that coincide with your initials, shuffle them whilst your eyes are closed, then opening your eyes place one at the beginning of your row of four cards and one at the end so that you now have a row of six cards.

It is now time for you to read your chosen cards which should help with the answer to your question or problem. Here is a sample reading to help guide you with your reading: After shuffling my two cards that coincide with my initials, the K was on the top and therefore first out so this makes it is the first card in the reading:

Card 11:
EXPECT THE BEST

You will receive what you expect to receive right now so expect the best.

The energies around you at this moment are exceptionally good but you will only get what you expect, so make the effort to expect the best and the effort will be made for the best to occur.

Next is your first card chosen out of your pile of sixteen and second in my row of six cards to be read:

Card 42:
WILL POWER

Use your inner strength and thoughts to draw all that is good towards you.

It only takes will power right now for you to stay on top. What we think we gain, whether it is good or bad, so use your will power to hold onto the good right now.

The following card is the first card out of the twenty six cards in the envelopes. (Remember though that you have added two cards to this pile from the last eighteen cards in the pack.) My first card happens to be one of these two. This is card three in your row of six:

Card 43:
WISH FULFILMENT

Any wish that comes truly from your heart is yours for the asking now.

Think hard about what your real wish is. Close your eyes and ask for the wish you need and want most right now and as long as it comes with love from your heart it will come true.

My next card is the second card from the twenty six cards in the envelopes, and now becomes card four in your row of six:

Card 21:
IS IT SPIRIT!

Your next dream will be a message from the person you love most in the Spirit World. Act upon it.

Your loved one is trying really hard to give you direction in your life. Please listen to your dreams then in effect you will be listening to the advice of the person you love most in the Spirit World. Listen to your next dream because it will indicate a way forward for you.

Now it's the second card chosen from the pile of sixteen to become card five in your row of six cards:

Card 44:
WONDER

All the good things are only around the next corner for you.

A wonderful future lies ahead for you because good things are only around the next corner where you are concerned. Your dreams seem uncertain but the back-to-front rule applies here, and they are definitely portraying good times full of wonder.

Last but not least is the first initial of my name from the pile of two. This becomes the sixth card in your row of six cards:

Card 10:
DREAM VIBRATIONS

Your dream vibrations are bringing a loved one in Spirit close to you right now.

Think of the person whom you most want to hear from in the Spirit World before you go to sleep for three consecutive nights. That person will appear in your dreams and Guide you forward in life.

Here are my chosen cards:

Card 1 = 11 = EXPECT THE BEST.

Card 2 = 42 = WILL POWER.

Card 3 = 43 =   WISH FULFILMENT.

Card 4 = 21 =   IS IT SPIRIT!

Card 5 = 44 =   WONDER.

Card 6 = 10 =   DREAM VIBRATIONS.
Have you noticed that already these cards read a story even though we only have the titles? With a word added here and there so that it makes sense, the story says:

Expect the best and with will power, wish fulfilment will be yours, making you think is it Spirit I wonder in my dream vibrations?

Now take the heading sentence on each card to lengthen your guidance story in its detail.

You will receive what you expect to receive right now so expect the best and use your inner strength and thoughts to draw all that is good towards you because any wish that comes truly from your heart is yours for the asking now.

Your next dream will be a message from the person you love most in the Spirit World. Act upon it because all the good things are only around the next corner for you and your dream vibrations are bringing a loved one in Spirit close to you right now.

So you see this does make sense when read as a story instead of just reading off the individual cards. If you want the full length version then put the information on the bottom part of each card together then it reads like this:

The energies around you at this moment are exceptionally good but you will only get what you expect, so make the effort to expect the best and the effort will be made for the best to occur. It only takes will-power right now for you to stay on top.

What we think we gain whether it is good or bad so use your will power to hold onto the good right now. So please think hard about what your real wish is. Close your eyes and ask for the wish you need and want most right now and as long as it comes with love from your heart it will come true.

Your loved one is trying really hard to give you direction in your life, so please listen to your dreams then in effect you will be listening to the advice of the person you love most in the Spirit World. Pay attention to your next dream because it will indicate a way forward for you.

A wonderful future lies ahead for you because good things are only around the next corner where you are concerned. Your dreams seem uncertain but the back to front rule applies here, and they are definitely portraying good times full of wonder. Think of the person whom you most want to hear from in the Spirit World before you go to sleep for three consecutive nights. That person will appear in your dreams and Guide you forward in your life.

I hope that this helps you to realise that it is worth all your effort to follow and go through this process, because if you do, it tells you in a clearly defined way what the answer to your question or problem is, and how to move forward to put it right. I thought that you may be interested to know that as I was writing the previous exercise something strange happened. I was using the computer to copy off my chosen cards to show you a sample of how to follow the exercise, instead of using the actual set of cards because they were not yet printed. During this process I accidentally copied card number sixteen by mistake, probably because my mind was thinking about the sixteen cards in one of my piles. Here is card number sixteen:

Card 16:
GOLDEN OPPORTUNITIES.

Your future is bright and you are going to have so many Golden

Opportunities to do well.

You are very lucky because your future is a very good one. All you have to do is grasp these opportunities with both hands as they come in your direction, and they definitely will.

As soon as I had realised that I had made this mistake I went back to where the pack of cards were and attempted to copy number forty two which was my chosen card but copied number twenty two instead. Here is card twenty two:

Card 22:
IT IS NOT THE RIGHT TIME

Do not hurry the situation just now because the time is not yet right for you.

It is your time to relax with the situation around you at this moment because it will all go wrong if you try to hurry things whereas, if you wait, your time will come and all will be yours.

I immediately deleted it and went back to where the cards were to find that now both cards sixteen and card twenty two had the writing about GOLDEN OPPORTUNITIES written on them. To sort this out I had to go to the edit button on my computer and keep undoing the previous action until the two cards had their original writing on them. But I came to the conclusion that because I do not believe in coincidences, this must be a message for me. Here are the three versions of my surprise message from Spirit:

Card 1 = 16 = GOLDEN OPPORTUNITIES.

Card 2 = 22 = IT IS NOT THE RIGHT TIME.

Card 3 = 16 = GOLDEN OPPORTUNITIES.

Says Golden opportunities are here but it is not the right time yet but the golden opportunities are definitely here.

The longer version is:

Your future is bright and you are going to have so many Golden Opportunities to do well so do not hurry the situation just now because the time is not yet right for you although your future is bright and you are going to have so many Golden Opportunities to do well.

The longer version of my message is:

You are very lucky because your future is a very good one. All you have to do is grasp these opportunities with both hands as they come in your direction, and they definitely will. It is your time to relax with the situation around you at this moment because it will all go wrong if you try to hurry things, whereas if wait, your time will come and all will be yours. Remember you are very lucky because your future is a very good one. All you have to do is grasp these opportunities with both hands as they come in your direction, and they definitely will.

I have repeated the first card at the beginning and the end because it came out twice in that order. Remember that if something is ever repetitive in your life it is a message for you to take extra notice of the subject that is being repeated for you. At the time that I was writing this chapter in the book I was waiting to hear about something that could prove to be important to my future and was wondering if I should make contact or not!! This message clearly tells me that the Golden opportunities are there and will be mine but I need to have patience and not try to force things along if I want them to happen. I naturally heeded this advice and it turned out that I was really glad that I did because it all turned out well and the Golden Opportunities were indeed mine.

Chapter Seventeen
Spirit and Humour

Students who are developing need to be aware of the fact that those in the Spirit World will sometimes use humorous ways to make a link to the living, therefore at these times they can show their opinion in a funny way. A classic example is when a close friend called Charles comes to visit me he always unties one of my shoelaces and reties it at the side of my foot instead of at the top where your shoes are normally tied, I now only have to show friends my foot and they laugh because they know that Charles has been to call. He had a wonderful sense of humour in life and we do not change the essential parts of our character when we die, hence his comical calling sign.

Whilst in Norwich working for Spirit, My husband Mike, Chris and I went into a pizza restaurant for something to eat because although Chris and I were dieting at the time, it was three thirty in the afternoon and all the other food places were either shut or short of food. I should add that although I was large and needed to lose several stone in weight, Chris was only eight stone eight pounds eight ounces "wringing wet", as the saying goes and even though Mike and I said that she did not need to lose any weight, she felt that she wanted to get back down to eight stone four pounds, therefore; she joined me with the diet. On this particular day as we went to fetch our food from the buffet counter, I saw Charles 'who is in the Spirit World and likes to play jokes,' grinning at us as Chris placed the final piece of food which was two cherry tomatoes on each of our plates. I smiled back and we returned to our table to eat our meal. Approximately five minutes later Chris tapped my arm and asked, "Have you pinched my cherry tomato off my plate?" I immediately retorted: "No I haven't touched your food!" She replied, "well it has disappeared! I have looked on the floor and every where and it is nowhere to be seen!" At that point Charles appeared and smiled again. I told Chris that I thought he was taking the micky about her being on a diet and had dematerialised the tomato for a joke. We all laughed about this and put it out of our mind that is until the next morning!

We went down for breakfast at the hotel where we were staying and Mike chose to have a full English breakfast so helped himself to the meal and went back to the table to eat it and look after our bags so that we could fetch our meal too. Taking our diet into consideration it was decided that we would have scrambled egg and mushrooms on two slices of toast each. Chris looked and said to me 'there is not enough scrambled egg, and at that precise moment a man turned up with a new container of freshly cooked scrambled eggs, to which I remarked: "You must be psychic. That is exactly what we wanted." He winked his eye and walked away. Chris placed four slices of bread onto the rotating toaster one slice at a time and we watched them go through and feed out through the bottom. As we do not like undercooked toast, she repeated the process but this time the fourth slice of toast never returned!!!

After several minutes of waiting in anticipation we called the man from before over, and he could not explain it either but suggested that we put another slice of bread in to see if it gets stuck on the one which must be lodged. However, that slice went straight through not only once but twice and I said to the man "I told you that you were psychic." He merely winked his eye once more and Charles suddenly appeared and winked his eye. We laughed at this and I told Chris that he was definitely taking the micky and was indicating that she did not need to diet. After breakfast we exchanged our calorie counters because Chris' had been working a lot slower than mine and we wanted to make sure that it was purely because I had so much more excess weight than she did that I was burning more calories. We returned to our rooms to get ready to leave and whilst I was brushing my teeth I saw Charles once more, he was winking his eye. Although this amused me I did not understand or ask him why he was doing this. But when we called at Chris' room on the way out, things became clear because she retorted "You would never guess what just happened!! I had just been to the toilet and was putting my clothes back together when suddenly my calorie counter jumped off my trousers and landed in the toilet."

Now we knew for definite that Charles was having a joke with us about Chris' excess weight or lack thereof. Incidentally I had worn my own calorie counter for three days and it had never jumped off anywhere let alone down the toilet. It did later dry out and was usable again and Chris did carry on with her diet, but Charles left us to it because he had made his point.

I think on that note it is time to get back to exercising your dream power through Spirit. Remember Spirits like Charles can communicate with Mediums like myself easily but it is not so easy to convey their message to most people. On this occasion you will also need a small piece of clean paper as well as your dream cards and notepad, which should once again be kept close to your bed. On your piece of paper write down clearly, the question in your life that you would like to be answered, in order to give you Guidance from the Spirit World, then prepare yourself ready for bed. Now hold the paper with the writing facing towards your chest, close your eyes and think about the question clearly for one or two minutes. After opening your eyes place the piece of paper on your bedside cabinet or near to your bed. For this exercise your pack of dream cards should be placed on your bedside cabinet or near to your bed and you should try to think about the question as much as you can whilst trying to go to sleep. (If your mind wanders it does not matter just turn it back to the matter in hand.)

On waking the next morning write down any dreams or waking thoughts into your notepad. It is important to do this because sometimes we think that we will remember and then it leaves our mind completely. The memory is a funny thing, it has a way of storing information away once we have received it, but unfortunately people cannot usually retrieve this knowledge easily. Also write whether the information that you are writing about came in dream-state itself or in your waking thoughts. (This will be important later on.) If you are racing about the next morning in readiness to go to work etc, leave the rest of your dream exercise until later in the day when you have more time to understand and appreciate the full meaning of your answers or lack thereof.

You may have noted that I said waking thoughts as well as memories of what you have dreamed? This is because those waking thoughts are usually those close to you on the Spirit side of life taking advantage of the fact that your semi sleepy state has placed you on the same vibration that they can communicate to you from. As soon as time allows for you to get back to concentrating on your dream exercise, sit and retrieve your dream notepad, cards and the piece of paper with your question that you are requesting help written on. Think as clearly as you can about the previous night when you were preparing to go to sleep including writing the question on your piece of paper and how you felt and indeed feel about the subject that you require Spirit's help with. As you are doing this take your dream cards out of the box discarding the packing to one side and slowly shuffle them until you feel that you are drawn to a card. Take it out of the pack and place it in front of you to the left hand side. Repeat this two more times, with the second card placed in the middle and the third card placed to the right as indicated below.

Card One   *Card Two*   *Card Three*

Now you are ready to see what your dreams are telling you. First of all may I say that with this exercise it does not matter if you feel that you did not dream the previous night. What matters is that you followed the instructions and went to sleep. This is because sometimes Spirit comes close to us during sleep state and instils us with peace because that is what is needed most at that moment in time, but they do not actually talk to us so therefore we do not remember having dreamed. In fact people who say they never dream are quite lucky because they are being taken care of and being filled with peace and love during their sleeping hours. Everyone dreams, this is a very necessary part of sleeping and I am sure that scientists would agree with me on this one. However Spirit feel that the rest, peace and love, is what you need most at that time, therefore they talk to you on a much deeper level, that is not easily recalled or remembered.

I believe that a lot of the time when people experience de'ja-vu it is in reality us recalling what we have been shown whilst in deep sleep state. We should pay a lot of attention to our de'ja-vu moments because you have visited these places and/or carried out these conversations in your deep sleep state because the incident is of some use to you on your life pathway. It makes sense to me that every living soul sleeps, dreams and experiences episodes of de'ja-vu at some point in their life. It is merely your Guardian Angel trying to show you direction. In actual fact it follows the same unwritten law as repetitive signs and signals. This is obvious when you give it some thought because it has to be repeated for you to remember or recognise it in the first place.

Read the question that you wrote on your piece of paper before going to sleep. For instance: 'Should I change my job, and accept the new one that I have the opportunity to take?'

Turn over card one and read its contents:

Card 6:
CELEBRATIONS

Congratulations it is now time for you to celebrate.

After a bumpy ride on life's pathway, things are about to go right for you. In order to have reason to celebrate, you need to be positive so that those good things that are now yours by right can draw near to you. Start to celebrate in your mind and heart in anticipation of these pleasing events, then it really will be time to celebrate.
Turn over card two and read its contents:

Card 21:
IS IT SPIRIT!

Your next dream will be a message from the person you love most in the Spirit World. Act upon it.

Your loved one is trying really hard to give you direction in your life.

234

Please listen to your dreams then in effect you will be listening to the advice of the person you love most in the Spirit World. Listen to your next dream because it will indicate a way forward for you.

Turn over card three and read its contents:

Card 31:
OPEN YOUR HEART

Send love from your heart to your enemies.

Give love to someone whom you do not like or are not happy with and you will reap great rewards. It is too easy to open your heart to those you love and are happy with, but more rewarding in the reverse.

The example cards above in correlation with the question; 'Should I change my job, and accept the new one that I have the opportunity to take?' are telling me:

Congratulations it is now time for you to celebrate. Your next dream will be a message from the person you love most in the Spirit World. Act upon it. Send love from your heart to your enemies.

If I was reading this in answer to the question: 'Should I change my job, and accept the new one that I have the opportunity to take?' I would take it to mean yes I should take the job when my loved one sends me my next message via my dreams, and that I should not be angry with those who made my present job difficult to handle but send them love which will help me to have reason to celebrate in my new job.

Can you see how easy it is? Obviously if you want to know more then you read the more in-depth reading from your three cards. If you have a dream from the previous night that you wrote in your dream pad, now is the time to look to see if there is any inclination towards answering the question you asked. Remember, that golden rule number one about analysing your dreams is that the human brain tends dream back to front and upside down, therefore quite often the dream means the opposite to what it is saying. I can actually feel you now posing the question: 'how will I know if this is the case?' Simple: If your dream is very stark and real as if you are actually living it, yet it does not make sense, then this is telling you that the dream is to show you direction. This is depicted by the fact that you are in fact the main character of the story unfolding but the story is jumbled up and does not make sense therefore it is obvious that this dream is being told in reverse order and needs unravelling. Whereas premonition dreams are more realistic and do make sense whilst living through the scenes within your dreams. You must also be aware that it is your own responsibility how you interpret your dreams and anything that you read in this book or any other is intended to be a guide and therefore cannot be held responsible for any wrong decisions that you make when responding to your dreams. The decision as to how you interpret is yours and yours alone. Although it is also true to say that the more you practice the easier it becomes to interpret it correctly. Remember also that any work with Spirit or your dreams is meant to have an element of fun involved with it because this is the right vibration to be on for you to get the right response from either of these important parts of life.

At this time Spirit are trying very hard to introduce Chris to ways of knowing when Spirit are with her and what they are portraying to her senses because this is very important if you are going to be a Medium. One Saturday we had arrived at a well known department store in Birmingham Town Centre and headed straight for the escalator because our first job on the agenda was always to have breakfast. Mike always laughs at us when we go shopping because he says that we have more coffee breaks than we do shopping. If we are honest he is right but I think it is a female thing isn't it?

Chris took my arm to steady me as I got onto the escalator because of my bad leg giving me the tendency to be unsteady at times, then as we went upwards an elderly gentleman who was approximately in his eighties climbed on behind us taking hold of Chris' arm as he did so. He remarked, "Seeing you two helping each other onto the escalator reminds me of my daughter when she was three. We lived in a bungalow because of our age, so she was not used to stairs so we had to show her how." By this time we had reached the top of the escalator and he disappeared off to the left as we went to the right. Chris and I turned to look at him but he had disappeared out of sight very quickly, especially for a man of his age!! Chris asked: "Was he real?" I just laughed because I knew that he was in Spirit so Chris replied: "He is Spirit!!! How would I know the difference?" I explained to her that firstly if you are unsure as to whether a person whom is talking to you is dead or alive, you need to pay attention to everything that is happening, even the seemingly small and insignificant things. Therefore these are the sort of questions she should have asked herself:

This man appeared suddenly as if from nowhere, so where did he come from? We had not seen him behind us before that point.

He was behaving in what seemed to be an unusual manner and he also held Chris' elbow very tight in a strange way.

Chris helped me onto the escalator yet he held her elbow and not mine.

Why did he tell us about his daughter and say: We lived in a bungalow because of our age, yet we had a three year old daughter so she was not used to stairs so we had to show her how."

Why did he disappear so quickly once at the top?
Was there anything else unusual about him?

Here are the simple answers to these questions:

The fact that he appeared suddenly as if from nowhere should always alert you to the fact that this person may be Spirit. If someone is behaving in an unusual manner you should always be suspicious of their motives for doing so. In this case the way in which he held Chris' elbow should have been a telling sign because he was holding her too tight. This is because he was drawing near to try to catch her attention and in doing so came in too close. This created pressure through the magnets within her aura, which in turn meant that the pressure of his grip seemed unduly strong.

He held Chris' elbow because although his conversation seemed to be aimed at the two of us, it was really directed at Chris. She should ask herself why, when I was clearly the one being helped.

He told us that 'his daughter was not used to stairs so we had to show her how,' even though we were not on stairs but on an escalator because he was saying that Chris needed to be directed forward in her recognition of Spirit. (You notice that he was not holding my arm) this was because I do not need directing forward to notice when Spirit are around.

He disappeared quickly at the top because he wanted her to notice the strangeness of what had just taken place.

His appearance and dress was a bit old fashioned for our time. But also isn't it slightly unusual that he needed to live in a bungalow because of his age, when he had a three year old daughter?

In all, the entire incident which lasted about thirty seconds could be described as strange and unusual. It is things like this that the budding Medium needs to look out for and pay attention to. I really believe that so many people do have glimpses of people in Spirit but just do not realise that they are in fact seeing dead people. Could this be you do you think? It is amazing how Spirit can help people to easily achieve something that they are generally struggling with. I was working in Redditch one evening and Chris had been with me on the journey. When we arrived back at my house at around midnight she said that she would need to attach her new Bluetooth to her mobile telephone (which she had bought that day after losing hers the night before.) before travelling home. The urgency was simply because she was very tired and if we came back late leaving her with a thirty minute journey home, still left to travel, I always telephone her and chat to make sure she stays awake and alert to arrive home safely, and we would never do this if the mobile was not hands free. Mike was in bed so we could not ask for his help so we sat on the sofa and set about working out how we could connect it for her. Chris kept on trying whilst I was giving her advice but each time it did not work. After about seven attempts I said: "Let me have a go?" She said that this would make no difference because I had been advising her all along. My instant reply was: "Well I attached the last one for you straight away didn't I?" At this she handed me her mobile and new Bluetooth to try. I attached them together straight away and handed it back to Chris smiling as I did so. She retorted: "How did you do that?" I just grinned and she commented: I know it was one of your 'Perks of the Job' wasn't it?" I had to admit that it was and she said that it was not fair because they did not help her. Whenever I am struggling with something I always ask Spirit to help if I have had a good try myself. It is at this point that they will usually help you because you have tried to help yourself. I call this a 'Perk of the Job' All of my friends know about my 'Perks of the Job'. I explained that they would have helped if she had asked and then listened to the reply. But let's face it they were helping her by letting me fix the problem that she had, weren't they?

Chapter Eighteen

Different Views of What Spirit Say and Do

It is interesting to see how differently people think and see things. What is straight forward to one is a complete jumble to another. This became very apparent one day when I was holding a demonstration at a book shop after the shop had closed. Everyone there had bought a ticket purely for the purpose of seeing me and hearing me Demonstrate my Mediumship. Because of this fact you would expect people to have some idea of what to expect and be ready for any eventuality in regards to what Spirit would say!! However, this is not always the case and here is a classic example:

I was giving a really nice lady a message from her loved ones in the Spirit World, which she was readily accepting until I said that the lady in Spirit had expressed that the lady receiving the communication had links to Germany. The lady immediately and quite adamantly said 'no' she did not have any links at all to Germany. I said that the lady in Spirit was quite sure but the lady once again said no. I repeated that the Spirit thought that she had and that they were usually right so was she absolutely positive that she did not have even a small link to Germany even though I suspected that the lady herself was Dutch. At this she said: The only link I have to Germany and that is not really a link, is that my daughter was born in Germany.

At this there was a huge sigh as laughter rose from the audience, as I explained that this was a link because technically speaking her daughter was German even though she was not in the country for long. She genuinely did not realise that this counted as a link even though it would be obvious to a lot of people. I suspect that the reason for this is because when we go to visit a Medium we have a tendency to tunnel vision into the people and information that we expect to come through for us. Therefore ordinary thoughts go out of the window.

At this the lady in Spirit told me to tell the lady here that she had died in England whilst she was in Germany giving birth to her daughter and the lady exclaimed "Oh goodness, yes she did!" So you see there was a very good reason for the lady in Spirit to bring up the link to Germany even though at the beginning the lady here thought that it was only a very tentative link. Because of the lady in Spirit plus my own perseverance the message was given as it was intended and did indeed offer proof of survival which is what we are all about.

One day I received a telephone call from a lady whom I have grown to consider a friend. She asked if it was possible for me to visit her six year old daughter who was having problems that connected to Spirit. I of course said that I would be delighted to try and help, as long as the Mother was present when I saw the young girl. We arranged a date and time and I arrived to see this young girl who I had not seen for about three or four years. As soon as I walked in and saw the six year old girl, I could not get over the striking resemblance to my grand-daughter Leah at that age. Unfortunately she did not remember her father personally because he had died before her birth, but through photographs and stories about her Dad that she had heard throughout her young life she felt as though she knew him well and loved him very much.

The main problem for her Mum at that time was that the little girl did not want to go to school or indeed be separated in any way from her Mother, Brother, Grandparents or other members of the family. She had been visiting a councillor but unfortunately this did not appear to be to helping with the situation at hand. She also talked about seeing her Father from time to time so that was when I was called in. We settled down to coffee and biscuits so that we could help the young lady feel at ease. (Although I am sure that most of you realise by now that I do not need an excuse to have a cup of coffee!) As we talked she became less shy. She talked about her Dad and why he had gone away and I explained to her that his disappearance from her life before she could meet him was in fact nothing to do with her. She had not done anything wrong. He loved her very much which is why he still comes to visit her. I then asked if she knew what happened when you die and she answered that "you go to Heaven where Spirit live." This made me smile and I told her that she was right. I asked if she knew why people die. She did not know so I went on to explain that every living person and animal has a soul which is their Spirit and that she had one just like daddy did. I also explained that when it is time our soul goes home to Heaven where daddy is, but it has to be our time and asked her once more if she understood?

She appeared to know what I was talking about and was smiling so I then told her that it was not Mummy's time yet so Mummy would not be going away. This brought a really big smile to her beautiful little face and I finished with, it is not time for you, your brother or anyone else you love to go yet either so you do not have to worry. Almost immediately you could see a change in her and I asked if she wanted to come upstairs with Mummy to show me her room. This was just a precautionary measure to make sure that when she said that she saw her Dad in her bedroom, that it was just that, her Father visiting his daughter. Her bedroom had a really good feel about it as did the rest of the house. I am sure that you could feel an amazing amount of love in their home, which in turn allowed Daddy to visit from time to time.

Her Mum asked her to tell me about the little Spirit man whom she had seen at her Grandparents home. She replied excitedly that a little Midget had come into her Grandparents home whilst she was there and told her that he was collecting his suitcases because he was going home now!!! When she told her Nan, she did not understand because as she explained there had only been one other family who lived in the house they now live in and they were still in touch with them, and he was definitely not a Midget, but a tall man, so therefore, she could not understand where this particular Ghost had come from?
I explained that the man had in fact never lived in her Grandparents house but had worked on the land where the house now is and had died there, and because Spirits haunt the space this had kept him there. He had told her that he was collecting his suitcases because he was going home now, because since she had been talking to her Dad in the Spirit World whilst at her Nan's home, it had allowed him to see the light which was the way home. So she had in fact helped this poor lost soul find his way home. The Spirit of this man had told the young girl in a way that he felt she would understand that he was going home to

the Spirit World and away from her Grandparent's house.

At that point her Mum asked if it was a small man, she adamantly replied no, he was a Midget. To which her mum said, "Could he be just a small man sweetheart?" She raised the palm of her hands towards the air, sighed and said: "No Mummy he was just a normal Midget." We laughed at this, because in the innocence and love that comes from a young child's mouth we were put in our place, and told in a way that any Midget would be proud of, that they are in fact the same as us just a different size, but we are all normal in our own way.

We then went down stairs for a coffee before I headed off home and whilst we were drinking it the little girl said out of the blue: "Mum can I go back to school after Jean has gone?" Her Mum hugged her and assured her that she could. This had come about because she was no longer afraid of leaving Mum's side in case she died whilst she was gone. She was also happy to have helped the 'NORMAL MIDGET' go home.

When practising to develop our God given ability to link with the Spirit World, like everything else in this life it goes in stages. People are always excited when they receive their first premonition because it is a definite sign that Spirit feel that they are ready to move on with their lessons. Chris was no exception to this rule. As usual she had lots of questions to ask when she found out that this was what had happened. She told me that she was certain that she was awake through part of what took place even though she may have been asleep during part of it too.

In her premonition Chris saw two high grass banks running parallel to one another, and if you look at it as though you are looking down a tube, at the end were the doors to a Spiritualist Church. There was a bench placed strategically on the embankment on either side of the Church doors. In the scene being shown to her, there was a man whom she knew in connection to a work issue, sitting on the bench to Chris' right as she approached the Church doors. In the scene that she was viewing he looked like a smart down-and-out who was wearing a large overcoat, when this did not appear to be his position in his real life.

In the scenes unfolding Chris and a person who is very important to her in life were walking up the grass bank on the way to the butchers, although it needs to be said at this point that in real life her butcher's shop is not situated in this type of surroundings. The man whom she knew, who was wearing the large overcoat in the premonition walked up beside herself and the person heading towards the butcher's shop with her. The important person in Chris' life asked: 'Are your Mum or Jean coming tonight?' Chris replied: 'no.' The man in the overcoat got down on his knees and laid his head sideways on the grass embankment near to where they were standing.

A girl who was standing further along the embankment shouted: 'Clear off.' At this the man in the overcoat clambered to his feet and started to chase after the girl. As he reached her they both tumbled to the ground with him landing on top of the girl. Both Chris and the person travelling towards the butcher's shop with her hurried up to the couple sprawled out on the floor and Chris called out 'Get off'. The man in the large overcoat had tight hold of the girl round her neck in a strangle hold, However, when the two ladies walked over to the couple on the embankment the lady who was being stifled by the man suddenly changed into Chris' dog Dougal who has been in the Spirit World for some considerable time now. The only difference being that Dougal's coat was now a lot greyer than Chris remembers it. Chris said adamantly: 'That is my dog!' At this the man in the overcoat let the dog go and Dougal ran to Chris.

This may seem quite complicated and hard to understand but here, by giving the story, followed by the meaning piece by piece, I will give you a breakdown of what the premonition is really saying:

Chris seeing the Church at the end of a pathway that ran in between two high grass banks running parallel to one another meant that she was now being carefully guided on her pathway towards her Spiritual

Development. The benches placed strategically on the embankment on either side of the Church doors, was indicating that there would always be time out to rest and consider. This meant for Spiritual comfort shown by a bench to take time out and reflect, leading from the right of the Church exit, or to deal with family or lifetime issues indicated by a bench to take time out and reflect, leading from the right of the Church exit. Seeing the man whom she knew in connection to a work issue, sitting on the bench to her right and the Church exits left, as she approached the Church doors in the scene being shown to her, was saying that this person is connected wholly on a here and now, or physical level and not a Spiritual one. (Shown by the side he was sitting.)

In the scene that she was viewing the man whom she knew looked like a smart down and out who was wearing a large overcoat, when this did not appear to be his position in his real life. This was telling her that he could not be trusted, he was not all that he appeared to be, this is indicated by his tramp like appearance. It was also telling her that she should be careful because he is clever and keeps his true motives in life well hidden. This could be read by the fact that he was smart, i.e.: clever and wearing a large overcoat, i.e.: covered up!!!

In the next scene, Chris and a person who is very important to her in life were walking up the grass bank on the way to the butcher's. Although in real life her butcher's shop is not situated in this type of surroundings. This was saying that her Spiritual pathway would direct her to avenues she has not travelled with the person who is indicated in her premonition and that they would wander closely through life whereas the past was behind her and Chris should not worry that it looked unlikely at the moment because things change. This is why her butcher's shop was shown in different surroundings to what she knows as normal. The man whom she knew, who was wearing the large overcoat in the premonition walked up to herself and the person heading towards the butcher's shop with her. The important person in Chris' life asked: 'Are your Mum or Jean coming tonight?' Chris replied: 'No.' The man walking up beside herself and the person she loved showed that there was something underhanded at work. The person asking: 'Are Your Mum or Jean coming tonight!' was indicating, that soon all will be back to normal because this is the type of question that you would expect to be asked, and Chris saying: 'no' was an ordinary answer for a normal question; making the point those things would indeed deed go back to normal.

The man in the overcoat got down on his knees and laid his head sideways on the grass embankment near to where they were standing. Once again it tells them to be careful because what you see is definitely not what you get. A girl who was standing further along the embankment shouted: 'Clear off.' At this the man in the overcoat clambered to his feet and started to chase after the girl. As he reached her they both tumbled to the ground with him landing on top of the girl. The girl 'who was a stranger to Chris' shouting at the man means that help will come to put the situation that is worrying her in life, right, from unexpected quarters. Him chasing the girl and landing on top of her means the culprit will do his best to stifle the truth from coming out.

Both Chris and the person travelling towards the butcher's shop with her hurrying up to the couple sprawled out on the floor and Chris calling out 'Get off' is shown, to indicate that Chris is also going to find the strength to speak up for herself, and those on the side of truth to do with the incident that is spoiling her peace of mind in real life.

In the premonition the man in the large overcoat had tight hold of the girl around her neck in a strangle hold, However, when the two ladies walked over to the couple on the embankment the lady who was being stifled by the man suddenly changed into Chris' dog Dougal who has been in the Spirit World for some considerable time now. The only difference being that Dougal's coat was now a lot greyer that Chris remembers it. This was because some time in the past Chris had similar problems and at the time she felt that Dougal was her only friend in the world because he did not judge her by what people said but believed in her for her merits. Therefore she was being told that the truth will out helped by friends here and in the Spirit World who will see the truth behind the lies being told. Dougal was shown as grey to indicate help from the past to the future. Chris said adamantly: 'That is my dog!' At this the man in the overcoat let the dog go and Dougal ran to Chris. This final episode of what is a premonition for good in the future says that Chris will state the truth with the help of other people and the person who is wrongfully lying about Chris and those connected to her will be found out for the wrong they have done, and Chris and the side of truth and Honour will win out in the end.

So I hope that this shows you how easy it is to understand what Spirit are trying to tell you if you break it down piece by piece instead of trying to work it out all in one go. It is the same when it comes to working out what Spirit are trying to tell you, whilst giving a message from them to someone here. So you see the answer is: do not, bite off more than you can chew, just give the message one sentence at a time like you would if talking to the living.

Dream
One evening shortly after this premonition took place, Chris had a dream that both pleased her and confused her at the same time. Here is the dream which took place as follows:

She dreamed that she was sitting in a lounge with me, my husband Mike and my daughter Toni. It was unclear whose lounge we were in because the furniture was positioned similar to all three of our homes. If you picture that there was a sofa and the two armchairs had been pulled up to either side of it positioned tilted slightly inwards towards the settee. My Daughter Toni was seated in the armchair to the left of the settee with Chris sitting at the end of the sofa next to Toni's chair, with me seated next to her on the settee. There was a gap and then Mike was sitting near the other sofa arm next to the empty chair, where my lap top that was in its case was on the floor leaning against the empty chair. We were all enjoying a plate of Spaghetti Bolognaise.
We were seated as shown below:

(Laptop standing on the floor leaning against the empty chair.)

(Toni in armchair)   (Empty armchair.)

(Chris - Jean —— Mike on settee.)

My laptop was in its case and standing on the floor leaning against the empty armchair.

<u>Analysis.</u>

It was reasonable that she did not know whose lounge she was in because where she was, was unimportant. This is because it was the events and the people present that were meant to teach her something and not the place where it happened. You may think that our seating positions and the meal itself were of little importance but it does tell part of the story. My daughter Toni was there, sitting closely to our left, and Chris was sitting close to my left whereas Mike was sitting with a gap between us. The reason for this is a simple one and hopefully one that will easily be understood.

Toni was close into our left and seated on a chair whilst the rest of us were on the sofa, when my Guides are situated to my right. This is so because although she will eventually develop her very strong gifts of linking with Spirit, it will not be for a while yet, even though she is starting to show more interest, (hence her part in the dream) which is a surprise to us all because she has always been afraid of Spirit. On the other hand Chris is sitting close to me on my left because her learning to link with and communicate with the Spirit World has already begun. She is seated next to me with Toni the other side so that she can be of help to Toni in her amateur status but this also means that she is not only sitting close to me, but also near to my Guides, who will also help her to advance. Mike however, is sitting with a gap between the three of us and himself. Those who know me well are now thinking: Mike always sat a little away from me when eating something like Spaghetti Bolognaise in case I have a spasm and he ends up wearing it. Although this is true, it is not the reason why he is sitting apart from us in Chris' dream. It is because Mike is already trained and as such does not require the help of myself or my Guides to the degree Chris does to push him forward in that way, yet he is in the dream and mentions the fact that Chris' Dad is there to show that he is around to help too should she need him.

The reason for the meal being Spaghetti Bolognaise as opposed to anything else is because to eat a meal like this you need to concentrate because it is not an easy meal to manage for some people. This indicates that to understand messages from the Spirit World you need to pay attention to the matter at hand as well as being in the present where you live your life.

Dream:
Chris suddenly noticed the laptop move, and was thinking that it could not have moved by itself, when the thought, Dad, came into her head suddenly. At this point Mike said out loud that it was her Dad, as she was thinking', Dad if that is you, please move it again', and the laptop fell over lying flat on the ground at precisely that moment. (Remember it had been standing upright on its side before this.) As she rose to her feet Chris looked up and she could see her Dad standing there, although he looked more like a sketch drawing than a real person. (Almost like a caricature.) She kept repeating: "I can see him. I can see him" and was crying. She sat down then stood up again. At which point I said", I can see him too", as I smiled towards her Father. Her Dad walked over towards her and gave her a hug and a kiss. She remembered feeling his hand on her shoulder, then the cold where his hand had been once he had removed it. Then as suddenly as he appeared he had gone.

Analysis:
When Chris saw the laptop move, it was her Dad who had moved it, and the fact that she straight away connected the incident to her Dad meant that she had indeed sensed his presence before she saw him. Mike told her that it was her Dad because he too had noticed his appearance in the room. (Once again it is being indicated that Mike will also be there to help Chris should she need it.) Her Dad slid the laptop

over onto the floor in direct answer to her asking him to move it again if it was him and to agree with Mike's statement that he had done it.

Because Chris had risen to her feet in excitement at this gesture in time, she had accidentally raised her vibration at the same time. This happens if we get overly excited; it is a natural occurrence. If this takes place frequently we very quickly learn how to change our vibration naturally without any form of excitement taking place first, after all practice makes perfect as the saying goes!!! At this point in the dream, Chris was crying and she sat down and immediately got up again. This indicates there will be free movement of her Spirit Work, with the tears suggesting her emotional happiness. Then at that point in the dream I had said: 'she can see him!!' and as she looked at me, I was smiling. This was me assuring her Guardian Angel who she calls Mr A for short (because his name is Mr Archbaldus,) that she could in fact see her father even though it was subjectively, (hence his sketch like appearance). I was smiling at him because he was indicating that he was very pleased with her progress. Chris only managed to see her Dad like a sketch drawing because she had only altered her vibration enough to see him subjectively and incidentally this is what they look like when we see them this way. I smiled in his direction to acknowledge to both Chris and her Father that he was there.

A hug and kiss from her Dad was indeed encouragement for her to carry on developing these gifts because they were the best presents that he could have given her. It is amazing that she could still sense the cold on her shoulder where his hand had been after he had removed it, because this said that she was developing not only how to see Spirit subjectively, but also how to sense when they are definitely there. He disappeared as suddenly as he had arrived because his job for that moment was done. His message had been passed across and received well.

I know that you are probably confused as to why this had to take place in a dream, but the answer is a simple one. In the beginning we tend to make excuses for things that we see and sense that are inexplicable whilst we are awake, so it is easier for them to progress us a little whilst in sleep state or between the two states of being awake and asleep at first. Chris tells me that she woke up after this dream feeling really happy and she is noticing more Spiritual events since then so you see he really has helped by visiting his daughter in her dreams.

As I was writing out the analysis of the above dream the lights dimmed to almost out just as I was changing a spelling mistake where I had put two N's instead of one in the word 'In' at the beginning of the sentence In the dream…….. Then as I was writing the end of that paragraph which said that: 'Chris' Spiritual Development was being worked on all the time' the lights came full on again. I took this to mean that I needed to point this fact out to Chris so that she knows that even when it looks as though she is not moving forward with her Spiritual Development, she in fact is. I did as I was being told and reassured Chris of this later that day when I saw her. Interestingly enough, when this book went to be proof read it turned out that this story was in the book twice, so you see Spirit were also trying to tell me something when they flashed the lights but I am afraid for the time being it had fallen on deaf ears.

Once Spirit decide that it is time for us to move forward, all sorts of things start to happen in order to get our attention. Sometimes these occurrences are small but make us sit up and take notice anyway. Here is one such occurrence: One morning whilst getting herself ready for work, Chris went into the front zip pocket of her handbag, where she kept her lipstick, to find that it was conspicuous by its absence because it was not there! This surprised her because this was where it was always kept. She immediately set about emptying the entire contents of her bag in search of the missing lipstick but this was also in vain. She then repeated this action twice more but to no avail. It was nowhere to be seen. Her next place to look was the drawer where she keeps all of her make up. At first sight she thought that she had found the missing item but unfortunately it was not. It was a different colour but as she was now running late she decided to wear that colour and set about applying it onto her lips. This done Chris opened the zip compartment at the front of her bag to place the new lipstick in, but lo and behold there was the missing lipstick! It had been in the front pocket of her bag all the time. Or had it? I know what I believe! Spirits are preparing her to go forward in her Development of linking with the Spirit side of life. Good eh!!?

I was in a Spiritualist Church giving a message to a lady in an aisle seat and Spirit went to the two ladies sitting directly behind her. This was okay because the people were together but then after going back to the original message recipient they decided to go to the two ladies sitting next to her whom I felt were not connected to the original message recipient and was right. I could not understand this and stated so because Spirit only usually swapped to another person mid message if they were linked together which as I said before they were not. Then a lady gave me her name Betty but I felt drawn back to the lady behind then a gentleman called Fred and a lady called Marjory also came through. I felt strongly that there was some sort of link between the three yet the lady said that although she could definitely take all three she was also certain that the couple did not know the Betty. I told them that it was really weird because when I spoke to her she kept directing as if I needed to look here within the Church yet I knew she was dead because she was speaking to me. I finally said there must be some sort of link to do with a Betty that joins the three plus yourself and Betty goes a lot further back to when you knew her. She answered well Fred and Marjory were a couple and they both died fairly recently but I knew Betty many years ago. I replied that seems to fit but why do I feel that Betty is here when she is clearly in Spirit? She immediately retorted because my name is Betty too. Problem solved.

Then I said I still do not understand why Spirit were changing mid message to talk to the other two people to which Spirit replied they will say that they do not know each other but they should look for the link between them because they will find that there is one. I repeated this and carried on with the next persons messages. After the service had finished and I was talking to people one of the ladies came up to me and said: Jean because of what you said to me I asked those three people if they would look at a photograph of my Mum to see if they knew her and to our amazement she used to teach them all dance lessons thirty five years ago. It never seizes to amaze me how Spirit sometimes work to get their message across and to get people here together and talking!!!

19
Our Choice to Follow
the Principle of
the Brotherhood of Man

Chapter Nineteen

Our Choice to Follow the Principle of the Brotherhood of Man

As soon as our soul is born onto the earth, we are destined to follow a certain pathway. The seven principles of Spiritualism are all to do with following that pathway in the right way so that our life journey is leading us in the right direction, Our second principle which is: the Brotherhood of man is very important from the word go because this is indicating to us that we should treat each person as our brother or sister because they are the same as us regardless of skin colour or culture.

When a baby is first born, that child will snuggle up to any living soul who cares to pick it up and bring love and warmth to her/him. This is because each person is born with the love in their soul to treat each person as their brother/sister. In other words it comes naturally to do so. It can however be dependant on who teaches us from that moment on whether we choose to care for our fellow man or go in the opposite direction which is the direction of hatred. These things are put in our way as lessons to see whether we are a good and Spiritual soul and have learned our lessons or not.

I am often asked why some people have greater advantages in life than others, if we are meant to treat each other the same because this difference makes the pathway ahead that we need to follow very difficult. For instance how can two people with the same brains and disposition, but one of the two comes from a poor background whilst the other is from a rich upbringing, do as well as each other?

First of all we need to be aware that these two people may be at the same level in the intelligence status, but spiritually they may be Worlds apart. I can just imagine that people reading this are now thinking that the person who is lucky enough to come from the rich background must be the one who is further ahead and therefore the more spiritual of the two. This however, is not necessarily so, or it may be the case. I know that I am probably confusing you now, but please read on.

The child born into the rich family is generally expected to go further because they have all the advantages that the poor person does not have, except for on rare occasions where the parents are not interested in pushing their child forward and may think that money will be all they need. Unfortunately this in itself can bring more pressure to bear because whilst more is expected of the majority of these people, they also have more distractions than perhaps someone would have from a poor background.

Those that are expected to think that the World is their oyster because they have money need to work really hard to stay on their spiritual pathway because their attitudes can become those of their parents and this is not the correct or spiritual way to be in life. They are also often taught that it is a dog-eat-dog type of World where you have to be on top because it is expected of you, just as it was your forefathers. This person can also be given the advantage of being able to take part in any type of sport or pastime that they wish to because they can afford to do so, and mostly they are not expected to work to earn their pocket money or pay for their way forward.

The poor person on the other hand, has to depend on the attitude of his or her parents as to whether they are pushed because it can be difficult for their parents to get the money together to pay for their child's private tuition, if the child is struggling in any direction.

Just because you strive in the world and do well does not always mean that you are a Spiritual being. I have indeed met doctors in hospital situations who think that just because they are in a very educated position in life this makes them better than the patients whom they are treating.

These people tend to take care of themselves and how much money they can earn, riding roughshod over their patients rather than go forward in the way of truth and love for their fellow man and treating these people with care. Remember their patients are men and women who do have feelings. What goes around comes around and as educated and lucky they may be to have more of the good things in life, they are not following the principle of the brotherhood of man, and will therefore find that the end result of their lifetime here on earth will not bring them as much pleasure as the hospital doctors whom I have had the fortune to meet that do indeed treat their patients like people with feelings, and listen to what they have to say without making snap decisions based on how busy they may be, and are not guided by how much money they can make.

These people will indeed have a very good entrance to heaven when the time is right because they followed the principle that is the natural law for man to follow and that is the Brotherhood of Man. Talking of that principle and the sixth principle which, says we will receive compensation and retribution hereafter for all the good and evil deeds done on the earth, reminds me of a very special young lady called Amy who is just twelve years old and is already proving to be very Mediumistic, 'just like all natural Mediums of her age'. She told me that her analogy of how to reach where Spirit resides was that:

"Above the clouds you would find that instead of the sky there would be the largest bar of chocolate (or whatever is most enjoyable to you,) that you are ever likely to see. This bar of chocolate for the sake of talking covers the whole of the earth above us instead of the sky and it would depend on how good you were in your lifetime on earth as to how big a bite of that chocolate you could have."

This would of course also mean that the better your goodness in the course of your life span here on earth, the bigger the space for your entry into the land of the Spirit World would be and therefore the higher the plain that you would be able to reach. And the more you would be able to communicate with those you love and have left behind. Obviously the bad people would only gain a small entry point so would not get very far at all, so therefore would remain on the lower plains and not meet up with those of us who try to do our best in life and be as Spiritual as possible." I personally think that this is a very good and simple explanation of how we gain entrance to heaven.

To a child or in deed a young lady like Amy it is more inviting than a gate that we all enter through, good and bad alike. Amy is indeed a very special young lady who has the most amazing goodness within her already at the tender age of twelve. She follows the principle of the Brotherhood of Man naturally in her life so will indeed earn herself a gigantic bite of that chocolate bar when the time comes for her to go home to the Spirit side of life. However, that is a long way off yet and she is already showing great potential to become a future Medium. Spiritually she reminds me of myself at that age.

As I told her when I spoke to her on the day of her twelfth birthday, I was exactly her age when I first realised that I was able to see and communicate with the World of Spirit, and had done so all my life. She told me that sometimes she would be sitting at home in her lounge and she could feel the atmosphere behind her buzzing as though lots of people had crowded into the room behind her. This is exactly what it feels like when Spirit friends and visitors come to join us. She said that sometimes when she felt a bit sad for any reason that feeling felt like a warm glow just as if someone was giving her a hug, and do you know, that is exactly what Spirit are doing. Good don't you think!!!?

Amy was also telling me about a building that she visits which is reported to be haunted. She explained that as you walk up the corridor to the top there are double doors to the right and to the left. If she turns to the right it feels normal but if she turns to the left she always feels sad. She is indeed picking up on the feelings given off by the ghost who is haunting that space and trying to tell its story of why they are there. Amy definitely is a future Medium in the making should she wish to take it up. I wish her all the very best in life whatever she decides to do because I do not wish to repeat myself but she is indeed already very much a very special and Spiritual person who has already earned herself a big bite of that chocolate bar called heaven. Good luck Amy.

Good night – sweet dreams!

ACKNOWLEDGEMENTS

I would once again like to give my sincere thanks to my husband Mike and my Personal Assistant and closest friend Chris Beech, who are always at hand when needed and who make my work a possibility because of their help.

These thanks also go to these special people: Amy, Andy, Cosie, Grace, Jeannette, Joanne, Nicola, Simone, Sue, Tess, and all at Biddles, for their input in making this book a possibility with their continuous support.

Many thanks to Andy Holmes, Doug Beaumont, Mary Wheeler, Phil Mcknight, Roger Parr, Roger Grafton, and Russell Grant for all that they do and have done.

Thanks also to Melvyn Holmes who designed the book cover of 'Dreamsteps to Heaven' based on the design by Jean Kelford.

Not forgetting a huge thank you to all my readers and supporters.

Jeans first book is: 'Oblivious But True.'

Jeans second book is: 'Is It You! Or is it Spirit?'

Both of the above books are still available from all good book shops, Amazon or directly, via contacting: info@kelfords.co.uk

Sittings are available subject to a waiting list. All e-mails will be answered in due course, or if you would like to see Jean at work or meet her personally then look on the web site diary which is continually added to: info@kelfords.co.uk

Please look out for Jeans next book, which should be out in a few months time.